DIFFICULT MOTHERS, ADULT DAUGHTERS

A GUIDE FOR SEPARATION, LIBERATION & INSPIRATION

KAREN C.L. ANDERSON

Published by Mango Publishing Group, a division of Mango Media Inc.

Cover and Layout Design: Elina Diaz

For permission requests, please contact the publisher at:

Mango Publishing Group
2850 Douglas Road, 3rd Floor
Coral Gables, FL 33134 USA
info@mango.bz

For special orders, quantity sales, course adoptions and corporate sales, please email the publisher at sales@mango.bz. For trade and wholesale sales, please contact Ingram Publisher Services at customer.service@ingramcontent.com or +1.800.509.4887.

Difficult Mothers, Adult Daughters: A Guide For Separation, Liberation & Inspiration

Library of Congress Cataloging
ISBN: (print) 978-1-63353-717-0, (ebook) 978-1-63353-716-3
Library of Congress Control Number: 2017959858
BISAC category code: BISAC category code FAM033000 FAMILY & RELATIONSHIPS / Parenting / Parent & Adult Child, BISAC category code OCC019000n BODY, MIND & SPIRIT / Inspiration & Personal Growth

Printed in the United States of America

Disclaimer

This book is dedicated to mothers and daughters and to painful generational patterns that want to be healed.

It is dedicated to all the women who have come before us, who sacrificed their spirits and their dreams because the world was not yet ready for them and not yet ready to value women as they are and as they wish to be.

It is dedicated to the fierce, wild, liberated women who will come after us.

"Whether you can still call your mother, or not, this book will inspire healthy, life-changing patterns in what is so often the most fraught terrain of our lives. It models and inspires grace, acceptance, forgiveness, and thriving. I can still call mine, and Karen Anderson's high dose of rational, and yes, magical thinking...has made all the difference."

—**Laura Munson**, New York Times and international bestselling author of *This Is Not the Story You Think It Is*, and founder of the acclaimed Haven Writing Retreats

"The work that Karen C.L. Anderson is doing with daughters in regards to their mothers is some of the most important work on the planet today. When we understand how influenced our minds are by what happened when we were growing up, we can then decide to let it go. In this book, Karen gives us the steps to do just that. I know from experience that this work is not easy, but it is by far the most important work I have ever done. Let Karen show you the way."

—**Brooke Castillo**, Master Coach Instructor & Founder of The Life Coach School

"A valuable read for anyone who has or had 'mother problems.' And there's a bonus: the strategies she suggests could be helpful in any close relationship in your life.

—**Marsha Hudnall**, MS, RDN, CD, President & Co-Owner, Green Mountain at Fox Run

The Matriarch Mare

The Matriarch Mare is calm because her boundaries are impeccable. Because she knows who she is—with clarity and equanimity—the other horses respect her. She does not let herself be influenced by another horse's fears or anxieties or aggression. She knows the right thing to do, based on her own internal signals, and she does it. She doesn't need approval or permission. She lives and breathes from a place of integrity and certainty, because of her strong and appropriate boundaries. As a result, she is relaxed and at peace. She belongs to herself. She has an undefended heart.

—With thanks to Martha Beck and Elizabeth Gilbert.

Katherine Woodward Thomas' contribution to the field of personal growth is deep and wide. Her work has influenced many of the thought leaders who have influenced me. I am grateful for and honored by her endorsement of my own work. Even more so, I am profoundly thankful for the groundbreaking work she has done in the world. Thank you, Katherine, from the bottom of my bottomless heart. ~ Karen C.L. Anderson

TABLE OF CONTENTS

FOREWORD

One of my earliest memories is of fiercely scribbling letters to my mother, which I'd quickly hide behind a small wooden bookcase in my bedroom. There were dozens of them stuffed into the small, narrow crack between the wood and the wall.

Rather than confessions of devotion and love, my writings were a rant of rage. Tear-stained confessions of wishing I'd never been born. To my strict mother, I'd say nothing directly. Yet behind her back, I'd let it tumble out messy, mad, and manic on the page.

One day, as she was cleaning my room, she stumbled upon the hidden missives. Unfolding and reading them one by one, I sat frozen in fear on my bed, barely breathing. When she finally looked up, her fiery, accusing eyes shot right through me.

She beat me with a wooden brush and sent me to bed without supper. I was eight at the time.

If you've picked up this book, it's most likely because you too have stories to tell. Perhaps you also had a mother who either neglected or engulfed you (or some crazy-making and confusing combination of the two). Maybe she covertly competed with you in ways that set you up to fail. Perhaps you felt undermined, undervalued, or undernourished by the one person in this world who was "supposed" to be your safe place. Perhaps you've been continually confused by all of the crazy-making double binds you've found yourself in time and time again. Perhaps you were made to feel unworthy, as though nothing you did was ever good enough, though you tried—year after year—to please someone who was, on some level, devoted to never being pleased.

In response, you may have felt handicapped as an adult woman by a nagging and pervasive sense of inadequacy or by a cavernous lack of confidence. If so, these feelings have likely been at the source of painful life-long patterns, such as giving your power away, self-abandoning, creating co-dependent relationships, isolating yourself, sabotaging your success, and failing to realize authentic happiness in life—and in love.

If so, then you've come to the right place.

This heartfelt guide, written by the brilliant Karen C.L. Anderson, will lead you step by step through the labyrinth, to the promised land of liberation. She herself has walked this gnarly path and found her way to true freedom. And now, in these pages, she lovingly shines a flashlight to help you follow in her footsteps, so that you, too, might find the same.

Though nothing that happened to you back then was your fault, it is now your responsibility to evolve. I wish we could just pay someone to do this for us. Yet, no one but *you* can set yourself free from the many ways you've unconsciously been perpetuating the traumas of your past in the present. The key is to take a radical stand, give up being a victim of your childhood, and become willing to see how you've been the one keeping these hurts alive—so that you can finally begin making different choices.

This is actually good news. Because it means you now have the power to graduate forever from living the story of not being good enough, being unworthy, or whatever term you identify with as the reason that your mother couldn't love you in the ways you needed to be loved. It means you can literally outgrow being the "you" you've been in relation to your sick mother. It means that you get to awaken to your authentic self, and be liberated to live a happy, healthy life, and to have happy, healthy relationships. You can have relationships that are no longer defined by the self you've needed to be in order to stay bonded to your mother, but which are grounded in wholesome qualities such as mutual respect, honor, trust, and true care.

We know, intellectually at least, that we're not limited by what's happened to us in the past. Yet, sometimes it's hard to believe, given how often we find ourselves repeating it. We, once again, get involved with people who make us feel inadequate, devalued, lost, and alone. As if we are those young girls, thrown back to our childhood homes.

The frustration and despair you may have felt as being unable to change, has been deep. You may even be wishing, hoping, and praying that your mother will finally change and see the brilliant woman that you are—that she will validate your goodness, intelligence, bravery and value. Believing that, somehow, she's the one who is holding the key to your liberation.

Despite this, there's more good news. Your mother doesn't have to change one bit for you to be free. Because the majority of your struggles today have little or nothing to do with her. If you're still struggling to become the worthy woman that you are in life and in love, it's most likely because you've been stuck with the "self" you created in consciousness in response to your mother's behavior. You've somehow been stuck in the persona she projected onto you, and limited by the story that you yourself internalized—and have been sourcing your life from for decades by now.

After all, the truth is, you are not your mother's daughter. You are you. An autonomous adult who is a creature of goodness, light, and love and made up of the magic of Life. A woman who has the ability to take what happened to her in the past, and transform it into greater wisdom, depth, and authentic love. You can now redefine who you are, and what's possible for you to create in this life, outside of your relationship with your mother. You also get to see this poor woman for who she really is. Just another vulnerable, somewhat confused person on this planet who was just trying to find her way, as best she could.

Make this book your best friend. Sleep with it by your bedside. Read it each time you're about to call your mother—to remind you of the power you hold to make that conversation go well. Ultimately, I encourage you to use these chapters to help awaken yourself to who you really are, and the possibilities you're holding for great healing, health, and happiness. Not in spite of all you've been through, but in many ways because of it.

—Katherine Woodward Thomas, New York Times Bestselling Author of *Calling in "The One": 7 Weeks to Attract the Love of Your Life* and *Conscious Uncoupling: 5 Steps to Living Happily Even After*

CHAPTER 1
LINEAGE

....

Lineage is important. I didn't just wake up one day and know what I am about to share with you. I've been doing my own work for years, and I will continue.

I've read many books and articles. I've taken many classes and workshops. I've studied and received certifications. And most importantly, I practice.

My most treasured mentors and teachers are Brooke Castillo, Master Coach Instructor and Founder of the Life Coach School, and Randi Buckley, life coach and creator of the Healthy Boundaries for Kind People methodology.

Others whose work and art deeply influence me, whose work I read, listen to, practice, reference, and am inspired by include:

- Maya Angelou
- Brené Brown
- Martha Beck
- Byron Katie
- Iyanla Vanzant
- Dr. Christiane Northrup
- Dr. Shefali Tsabari
- Pema Chödrön

- Debbie Ford
- Bethany Webster
- Lynn Forrest
- Katherine Woodward Thomas

Additional information about these and other resources can be found in the *Recommended Resources* section at the end of this book.

CHAPTER 2
A NOTE TO DAUGHTERS...AND THEIR MOTHERS

O ne of the biggest patriarchal lies is that of the "perfect" woman (and it, obviously, includes mothers and daughters). This lie is the cause of so much intergenerational pain, dysfunction, and violence.

If you are a mother who is struggling, who worries that maybe you are a "difficult mother," the good news is that your daughter cannot ease your pain with her validation or her forgiveness. Why is this good news? Because you don't have to rely on her to feel better. What I wish most for you is the ability to validate and forgive yourself.

If you are a daughter whose mother was unwilling or unable to be who you needed her to be, my heart goes out to you. I'm guessing that deep down inside, without realizing it, she was terrified of being burnt at the stake, drowned, or stoned (whether literally—like women were centuries ago—or figuratively like they are today) for not being perfect as defined by others. This is collective trauma.

The unconscious fear and collective trauma can be what causes a mother to become abusive, addicted, or mentally ill...or to simply squash her daughter's desires to express and be her true self. It's not necessarily the trauma itself, but rather the belief that trauma is shameful and needs to be hidden that destroys lives.

So you may be wanting an apology or an acknowledgment that may or may not come. Or you may believe there's nothing your mother could ever do or say to undo your pain.

The good news is that your mother cannot ease your pain with an apology. Why is this good news? Because you do not have to wait for her apology to feel better. If you believe your happiness is only possible as the result of your mother's admission of guilt, she still has power over you. What I wish for most for you is the ability to take yourself on to your own lap and ease your own pain.

As women we have access to an infinite collective maternal energy that encompasses kindness, fierceness, compassion, and wisdom and it's *that* which gives us the ability to re-mother ourselves.

Take my hand...

CHAPTER 3
WHY I DO THIS, PLUS
FAQs AND AN INVITATION

· ·

I wrote this book because I spent many years suffering, struggling, and hating myself, all because I had a story about my mother, myself, and our relationship. I've been freeing myself from that story ever since. Of all the hard things I've ever done, this has been the hardest—and most rewarding, powerful, and liberating.

That is my number one credential. I have been there.

So what can you expect? This book is part lessons and concepts and part real-life experience. It's also part journal prompts and exercises that will help you apply the lessons and concepts and make them real in your own life.

I suggest you keep a journal specifically for this work. Why? Because writing is powerful and it's good for you. Writing about stressful events helps you acknowledge, cope with, and resolve them, which has a positive impact on your health.

Writing also helps you to:

- Clarify your thoughts and feelings. As you get deeper into the book you will understand the difference between the two.

- Know yourself better. What makes you happy and confident? What situations and people are challenging?

- Reduce stress. Writing about uncomfortable thoughts and emotions is the beginning of being able to release them.

- Solve problems from a more intuitive, creative place. Writing unlocks creativity and intuition, and unleashes unexpected solutions.

- Integrate what you're learning. It's one thing to consume information; it's another to act on it.

It takes courage to do this work. Intense emotions may come up as you make your way through the book. You might find yourself feeling everything from guilt to anger to grief, but also joy, hilarity, and relief.

How you feel about your mother right now is okay. Although there may be societal, cultural, and family taboos in regard to the emotions we experience in relation to our mothers (especially if those emotions are "negative") there are no taboos—or judgment—here.

The key is to engage with compassionate objectivity and examine yourself with fascination and curiosity, rather than harsh judgment, shame, and guilt.

To break in your journal, consider an intention for yourself as you work your way through this book. No matter where you are in your relationship with your mother, whether she is alive or not, whether you speak to her or not, consider three things when coming up with your intention:

- How you'd like to feel on a day-to-day basis.
- What you'd like your relationship with your mother to look like.
- Who you want to be and how you want to show up, not just in this relationship, but in the world.

And remember: this work is more about you than her.

FAQs

"What's different in this book as compared to *The Peaceful Daughter's Guide to Separating from a Difficult Mother*?"

In the two-plus years since the *The Peaceful Daughter's Guide* was published, several things have happened:

I've received hundreds of questions from women all over the world, some of which I've answered on my blog and in my newsletter. I've coached hundreds of women around their mother stories. I've come to understand the concept of boundaries in a much deeper and more nuanced way and have led Impeccable Boundaries workshops, both live and online. I've communicated with mothers who want to have better relationships with their daughters. I've explored my own stories on a deeper level and have consciously transformed some that were hurting me.

In addition to the core concepts laid out in *The Peaceful Daughter's Guide*, here's what you'll find in this book:

- More deeply personal stories and lessons
- More writing prompts and exercises

- A chapter dedicated to questions and answers, advice-column-style
- More resources for healing and thriving
- The incorporation of concepts from the Healthy Boundaries for Kind People methodology created by Randi Buckley

How do I know if I have mother issues (beside the obvious indicators like chronic conflict, lack of boundaries, or consistently feeling anxious or angry when I think about her and my relationship with her)?

Here are some common ways it shows up (in my own words, but with thanks to Bethany Webster): You compare and despair. You feel stuck, overwhelmed, and like an underachiever. Or you are overachieving, but without any joy or fulfillment, just going through the motions in an effort to prove your worth. You encounter issues such as:

- Shame, blame, guilt, and desperation
- Fear of failure
- Fear of success (believe it or not!): believing that if you succeed you won't be loved, someone will disapprove, or that you're somehow "showing off"
- Putting up with bad behavior in others
- Constantly seeking approval, validation, and permission from outside yourself (and especially from your mother)
- People-pleasing and being afraid to say "no"
- Taking on other people's problems and thinking it's on you to fix them

- Self-sabotage (especially when you get close to achieving something)
- Binge eating, binge drinking, binge shopping, binge anything
- Trying to control the uncontrollable
- Chronic worry and anxiety
- Believing that it is selfish or narcissistic to put yourself first, or even to love, accept, or care for yourself
- Believing it is your responsibility to take care of others, emotionally speaking
- Thinking that your desires and preferences don't matter
- Not having a clear sense of who you are and what you want
- And if you *do* know what you want, feeling incapable of doing or having it
- Having weak or nonexistent boundaries
- Being afraid to speak your truth and take up space

If you identify with any or all of these, it's not bad news. You may believe that this is just the way you are—that it's set in stone and unchangeable. Or maybe you understand that you can change it, but it feels overwhelming and near impossible to do so. Besides, you might not have had a great role model for being the woman you want to be. I used to feel the same way, until I learned (and more importantly practiced) the concepts I lay out in this book.

Does my mother have to be alive in order for me to get something out this?

No! This book and the lessons, concepts, and exercises aren't so much about the two of you as they are about you making some choices about how you want to show up in the world. This is about your future, and not just in relation to your mother (whether she's alive or not).

I don't want to have to talk to / see / interact with my mother. Are you going to suggest that I should?

Absolutely not. For some women, choosing to not have their mothers in their lives is the very best choice. What I want for you is to have made choices from a loving, proactive, powerful place, not from a reactive, defensive place.

My mother was abusive and violent when I was a child. Am I supposed to forgive and forget?

This book isn't about putting up with or approving of any type of abuse, whether it happened long ago or is happening now. It's about learning how to tell the story about what happened in such a way that it doesn't hurt or minimize you, but rather empowers and liberates you. It's about learning how to establish impeccable boundaries so you can put a stop to the abuse, if it is still happening.

I've taken everyone else's advice for years to no end. You can't possibly know my mother!

My job isn't to tell you what to do. My intention is simply to guide you in having your own back...in learning how to trust yourself implicitly when it comes to your relationship with your mother—or anyone else.

How is what you do different than therapy?

Therapy and coaching can coexist beautifully together, but their approach and focus are different.

1. Most therapy is diagnostic and clinically treats people with psychological disorders or mental illness. Coaching can pick up where therapy ends and starts with the premise that the client is okay and full of potential. Coaches do not diagnose or treat mental illness.

2. The goal of therapy is to take people from a dysfunctional state to a healthy, functioning state. Coaching helps highly functioning people get to the next level so that they can have a more meaningful and satisfying life.

3. Most therapy is focused on the past, using childhood to explain current problems. Coaching focuses on the present, the future, and the belief that you do not need to continue focusing on the past in order to feel better and move forward.

4. Therapy asks "Why?" As in, "Why do you think, feel, and behave the way that you do?" Coaching asks "What's next for you? How do you *want* to feel? What obstacles are standing in the way of you feeling that way?"

5. Therapy is usually a long-term process. Coaching is typically short-term.

6. Therapists are licensed professionals in a highly regulated industry. Coaches are not.

7. Therapy assumes the therapist is the expert. Coaching is an equal partnership.

Speaking from my own experience: therapy helped me identify the "pathology" of my past ("Your anxiety might stem from having a narcissistic mother."), which was helpful, but I continued to believe that my capacity for joy and my potential remained impacted by my mother. That it would be a "sad reality" for the rest of my life.

My experience with coaching showed me that I could choose otherwise, but I had to be ready to hear this. Coaching helped me take responsibility for my future. When we have dreams/goals and are having a hard time fulfilling them, it's often because we still have unconscious stories we're telling ourselves about what is possible.

AN INVITATION

How can I work with you?

If you've been through the therapy and have read all the books—if you're done looking back with dread and want to look forward, focus on what's possible, and have fun while doing it—I invite you to join *Mare: A Re-Mothering Community* (https://www.kclanderson.com/mare-community/). It's like an interactive advice column that will help you practice and integrate what you've learned ("make it real") and help you take those next steps you say you want to take, cheer you on when you take them, and hold your hand when things don't go the way you wanted them to.

Mare: A Re-Mothering Community is...

- a space where women who have read (or are reading, or who want to read) *Difficult Mothers, Adult Daughters: A Guide For Separation, Liberation & Inspiration* can gather to share their stories, practice the tools, and get support and coaching from me;

- a *secret* Facebook group;

- weekly writing prompts;

- access to my Impeccable Boundaries For Your Life & Relationships eCourse; and

- monthly recorded group coaching calls via Zoom; and a place where you don't have to go it alone.

At the very least, I encourage you stay in touch. The best way to do that is to subscribe to my weekly love note https://www.kclanderson.com/subscribe/.

CHAPTER 4
LIVING IN EITHER/OR LAND

· ·

W hen it comes to your relationship with your mother, does it often feel like an all-or-nothing, either/or proposition? Maybe you feel that you have to either be defensive, resistant, and protective of yourself, or instead just roll over and let her do and say whatever she wants.

Or maybe it feels like you either have to keep your conversations shallow and surface-y or go right into the emotional deep end.

Then there are times when you think you either have to shut her out of your life for good or allow yourself to be enmeshed with her forever.

None of these options feel good. In fact, just thinking about it wears you out.

Having felt this way in my relationship with my own mother, and having worked with other women on this issue, I find it's more common than you may think to feel this way.

At the very least, it's slightly annoying or limiting. At the very worst, it's intense and can feel as debilitating as impotent rage. And underlying all of it is sadness, and maybe unspoken grief.

I spent years in either/or land. Way back when, if someone had told me that it didn't have to be this way, I'd have simply said, "You don't know my mother." It felt like an intractable situation, with no pleasant solution.

Now I know better. I know there are infinite choices available, not just all-or-nothing decisions. There's immense freedom, peace, and sovereignty that comes with knowing this, along with being confident in making choices that feel good and right (and when I say that, I don't mean making choices for your mother's sake, for avoiding conflict, or for her approval).

So when it comes to your relationship with your mother, this I know for sure: You are not as powerless as you feel, and you can make choices that feel good and free.

I've been accused (mostly by mothers) of trying to push the wedge deeper between adult women and their mothers. I've also been accused (mostly by adult daughters) of not going far enough to promote "no contact."

If you are emotionally enmeshed with your mother, or if your mother was distant, disengaged, and critical, I wrote this book for you. You have little autonomy (the ability to make an informed, un-coerced, non-reactive decision; the freedom to be who you are, apart from your mother) because you believe (perhaps unconsciously) that your mother's opinions, needs, values, and desires are more important than your own.

Or you fear, on a primal level, what will happen if you choose to belong to yourself rather than belonging to your mother.

My hope for you, as you read this book, is that you learn how to belong to yourself—how to be your own woman emotionally separate from your mother.

That you come to understand that the only person you need to take emotional responsibility for is yourself.

That you discover that when you focus on *you*—on your values, desires, needs, and preferences—something magical happens: the way you show up in your relationship with your mother (whether you choose to see or speak to her or not) changes in a way you never imagined possible.

That you no longer tolerate abuse and engage in dysfunctional behavior.

That you trust yourself to have and hold your boundaries, not from a defensive, reactive place, but from a solid, grounded place.

And there's nothing more kind and respectful—to both of you and to women everywhere—than that.

Where most of us get caught up is in believing that words like "separate" and "connected" are emotions. These words do not actually express emotion, they describe thoughts, opinion, and interpretation, which, when you think them, create emotion. They express how you interpret others rather than how you feel. It's your interpretation that creates the emotion.

This is a crucially important distinction to make, because if you are using words like these to describe emotion, you will inevitably experience powerlessness.

When you're emotionally enmeshed with your mother, you doesn't know where your thoughts and emotions start and hers end.

She believes that in order for her to be happy, you have to think, feel, and act a certain way (so you don't know what you really think and feel, or how you want to be).

You believe the same thing: that in order to be happy, she has to think, feel, and act a certain way.

She has a tendency to think she knows how you feel based on how she feels.

You have a tendency to think you know how she feels based on how you feel.

I believe that true connection is somewhat of a paradox. It's possible when you and your mother are individual, autonomous women with your own thoughts, emotions, dreams, and desires. When you know, love, and trust yourself and she knows, loves, and trusts herself. When you are able to establish loving boundaries based on what you know, love, and trust about yourself and when she is able to do the same. When the two of you let each other be who you are, the good, the bad, and the ugly.

The good news is that your mother doesn't have to participate. She doesn't have to know, love, and trust herself the way you do or the way you think she should.

The more connected you become to yourself, the more open you can be to connection with her, no matter where she is on her journey.

Emotional separation from our mothers is the solution and the medicine, not the thing that needs to be fixed or healed. We don't need to "make peace" with it because it *is* peace.

CHAPTER 5
AWAKENING

••

The image is vivid in my memory. My mother is standing in the front yard and she's holding a letter in her hand—a letter she's about to put in the mailbox.

She holds it up, and declares, "I'm divorcing my mother!"

I was in my early twenties and she was in her mid-forties. I certainly wasn't surprised; it was no secret that she and my grandmother didn't get along. My mother often said that she would never treat me the way her mother had treated her. I'd heard the stories and they made me hurt for my mother.

Like the time my grandmother said to my mother, who had been voted the "Prettiest Girl" in her high-school class, "If I'd had more money, I'd have gotten you plastic surgery to fix your face." She told me that story several times and I know she was hurt by it.

My grandmother was a stunner. As was my mother. And like many, many women of their generation, their looks were everything. Their appearance and sex appeal (but not too much) was their currency. And deep down in the primal part of their brains, it was how they believed women survived.

I remember the first time I felt that there must be something wrong with my body. I was about eight or nine years old and had been to a pediatrician visit with my mother. When we got home, she said to my stepfather, "The doctor said she's chunky." I heard amusement, fear, and disgust all at the same time.

My mother put me on a diet when I was twelve. And when I reread the diary I kept during my high school years, it's filled with pages where I write about feeling like a pig, about hating myself because I ate too much.

Both my mother and my grandmother were concerned about my weight, and when I look back at photos of myself then, all I can do is shake my head. I didn't have a "weight problem." What I believe now is that she was worried about two things, one consciously and one unconsciously. First, she was worried about what others would think about her if she had a fat daughter; secondly, she worried that if I had a fat body, then a man wouldn't love me and take care of me.

* * *

As a young adult I believed my mother and I had "typical" mother-daughter conflict, but I also thought our relationship was different—better than the relationship she had with her mother. My mother often said that we were close—good friends, even. I know she wanted it to be different between us than it had been for her with her own mother.

What I didn't know at the time was that my mother and I were not "close"—we were codependent and emotionally enmeshed. We were both single and we'd go out to nightclubs together and drink, flirt, and dance with men who would cleverly suggest we were sisters. She was involved in almost all aspects of my life and when I wanted to keep some things separate, she would be hurt and/or angry. And because I craved her attention and approval (unconsciously), I did as she wanted.

I didn't understand how unhealthy our relationship was.

Fast-forward twenty-five years, at the end of 2010, and there I was, divorcing my mother, too. Instead of a letter in the mail, I sent her an email. Despite her (our?) desire for a different, healthier mother-daughter relationship, it appeared we couldn't escape those etched-in-stone patterns. My mother had unconsciously passed down attitudes and behaviors, I unconsciously took them, and when I wanted to strike out on my own and have a life separate from my mother, our relationship suffered.

I will tell you about some of the things that led up to that moment—the things that I believed justified "divorcing" my mother—but what's important is to know for now is that in that moment I felt like I had no other option. I believed that divorcing my mother—choosing to have no contact with her—would solve all my problems.

Instead, I found myself obsessing about our relationship. To anyone who would listen, I'd pour out my hurt and anger, sharing the details of how my mother had done me wrong. I was operating from an unhealthy, unconscious belief that I was my mother's victim.

When I discovered the concept of victim consciousness, it all made sense. Up until that point, I resisted the idea that I might be a victim because in my family, "being a victim" was something to be ashamed of and to avoid at all costs. I highly recommend the work of Lynne Forrest and her book *Beyond Victim Consciousness* for fully understanding this concept, but let me lay out the basics here.

Imagine an inverted triangle. At the bottom of the triangle is the Victim, in the top-left corner is the Persecutor, and in the top-right corner is the Rescuer (note that both these roles are in the "one up" position from the Victim).

When we're in victim consciousness, we're playing one of those three roles, and it's important to recognize that none of these roles is considered better than other (especially when everyone in the dynamic is an adult). The Rescuer is not the "good guy." In fact, the Rescuer and the Persecutor are basically exaggerated versions of the Victim.

This dynamic plays out on a micro level in families, and we can also see it playing out in the world, on a macro level.

According to Forrest: "Victims think of themselves as weak and unable to take care of themselves, so they are constantly on the lookout for someone to rescue them. Rescuers tend to believe that their own needs are irrelevant. They believe that they matter only when they are taking care of others, and that means they constantly need someone to take care of. Persecutors believe the world is a generally unsafe and fearful place. They think of themselves as being in constant need of protection from a world that is out to get them, and so they get angry at others or at situations believing that they are only defending themselves."

No matter where you start out on the triangle, you will eventually play the other two roles. If you're the Victim, you start to feel resentment, and may even move into the Persecutor role in order to change the pattern, believing you are protecting yourself. Or, you may move into the Rescuer role in order to feel important because you're taking care of the Victim.

In hindsight, I see that my mother and I constantly revolved around the triangle, each of us playing all three roles.

Shortly after I "divorced" my mother, I became my maternal grandmother's legal guardian. Given that her children lived in other states (and in one case, in another country), it made sense that I, who lived about ninety minutes away, take on this role. Not to mention, as I said earlier, the relationship between my mother and her mother was strained.

When it became obvious that she'd no longer be able to live alone in her home, I moved her into a skilled nursing facility, cleaned out her house, and sold it. It was while readying her house for sale that I found a series of letters she and my mother had written to each other, from the time my mother was eighteen and in college.

I treasured those letters because they gave me so much insight. They mirror, almost exactly, some of the correspondence my mother and I have exchanged over the years. In some cases, the letters conveyed basic day-to-day observations and news, but other letters were filled with rage, hurt, accusations, and confusion.

I even found the famous "I'm divorcing you" letter my mother sent my grandmother.

My point in sharing this is to illustrate that despite what we say, despite what we might intend, what we model is what makes the biggest impact. I'm not saying I divorced my mother because she divorced hers, nor am I saying that what either of us did during that time was right (or wrong). Dysfunctional patterns, if not noticed and acknowledged honestly, get passed on.

Although I chose not to have children, I saw the effects of those patterns in some of my other relationships, from my marriage, to my sister (same father, different mother), to my stepkids. I was harsh, critical, controlling, and downright mean sometimes. I believed I was justified. I was treating others the way my mother had treated others, the way she had treated me...and the way I had treated myself. Being "in conflict" was the norm. I was used to it.

I'm not blaming my mother, or her mother, for the patterns. What was passed down was the unconscious pain of being a woman in a culture that does not equally value women. This is the pain of "not good enough" and of harsh self-judgment, criticism, and unworthiness.

This pain has been passed down, woman to woman, mother to daughter, for centuries.

They told us "just be yourself," but they taught us (via example) to be someone else. Conform. Standardize. Comply. Obey. And if we didn't, we were often accused of being selfish, or being a show-off.

Think about it for a second. Centuries ago, women were burnt at the stake, stoned, and drowned (literally and metaphorically) for being their true selves, for expressing their true selves. Especially when that self was deemed to be evil, magic, wild, intuitive, inappropriate, too sexual, too thin, too fat, too much, too smart...you get the picture.

Fast-forward to the beginning of twentieth century and instead of being murdered, women were labeled as "hysterical," thrown into institutions and locked away, told that it was for their own good.

Today? The murdering and locking away still happens, especially to women of color, but mostly it takes the form of being shamed, harassed, and threatened in the media.

It makes sense, then, that our mothers (and grandmothers and great-grandmothers), scolded us for being anything that might make us unattractive or ineligible for marriage, because for most of history women could not survive on their own.

Thus, generation after generation, women have had two universal (and often unconscious) conflicting needs: (1) I must be my true self...I must express my true self. (2) I must protect myself from being burnt at the stake, so I will squash and mold and contort myself so I "fit in" and am deemed "okay."

So of course our mothers felt the need to protect us, while at the same time trying to model independence, while at the same time trying to protect themselves, while at the same time being pressured to "do it all"—perfectly— while at the same time, perhaps, turning to addiction or becoming mentally ill or, maybe, just being jealous and pissed off.

By itself, this generational pain is one of the most significant sources of dysfunction in our relationships. Those beliefs and patterns are running in the background of our lives, and we often have no clue that they're there at all. We just know that we're not as content as we'd like to be. Our relationships aren't fulfilling and rich.

The good news is that we don't have to take what is handed down. It's not something to blame our mothers or fathers (or ourselves) for, it's something to understand, accept, and work on. Meanwhile, we come to know that we can do hard work without suffering—that it can be one of the most joyful, affirming things we ever do.

By being honest and aware of how, at first, I chose to believe that I was not good enough, I opened the door to healing. In deciding that I didn't want to believe it any more, I released it, not just for me, but also for my mother, her mother, and on and on, and walked through that door.

Doing this work heals—not just you, and not just in the present—but also past generations (although I believe doing it just for you is perfectly okay). It also changes the future for the better.

When we choose to focus on and heal our mother stories, we transform them from something that wears us out and causes us to suffer into something that is a source of wisdom, creativity, and peace. We go from believing we should be happy all the time to being alive and awake. We go from thinking we're broken and needing to be fixed to knowing we're complete and whole *as is*.

And that is the number-one reason to take an honest and compassionate look at your relationship with your mother and to ask yourself what you've chosen to take from her and what you're passing on, and if it's not what you choose, then to heal it.

World peace does indeed start inside each and every one of us.

CHAPTER 6

"SO, TELL ME ABOUT YOUR RELATIONSHIP WITH YOUR MOTHER."

C lassic, right? It's what every therapist I've ever seen, traditional or alternative, has (eventually) asked when I sought help for various issues (from weight loss to anxiety).

And then there are all the books I've read. Books about toxic families and "bad" mothers.

While I found great comfort in telling my story to therapists, and in realizing that I am not alone when I read those books, none of this insight or experience did anything to bring me true and lasting freedom and peace. And that's not the therapists' or books' fault.

While identifying and understanding our mothers' issues is helpful in being able to provide context for pathology, it doesn't always give us a path forward. It can actually limit our growth and potential.

It can be a relief to have an explanation, but it can also validate us in feeling angry, sad, bitter, disappointed, and reactive. On one hand, it felt good—exhilarating even—to tell negative stories about my mother in the various online "support" groups I discovered, and to read other women's similar stories.

On the other hand, those groups seemingly supported me in staying a lesser version of my self, which, ironically, is often what happens between mothers and daughters. So many women share that it's only when they're struggling that their mothers seem to pay attention, and when they're thriving, their mothers display a range of behaviors— everything from ignoring them to lashing out at them.

I experienced something similar and then went deeper into an unhealthy "blame" mode because I believed it shouldn't be this way.

My mother shouldn't have been the way she was, I shouldn't have been the way I was, my parents shouldn't have gotten divorced, and all the bad things that happened in the past shouldn't have happened.

There is no freedom or peace in shoulds and shouldn'ts.

While I didn't like feeling angry, sad, bitter, disappointed, and reactive, those emotions were validated by experts, therapists, support groups, and books (and friends and family), so I thought I had a good reason to feel them, but not for the rest of my life!

Therapy, self-help books, and support groups provide a justification for our pain; in my case they also provided a justification to stay a lesser version of my possible self. The unconscious belief many women live from is "My mother is a [insert personality disorder, mental illness, or addiction here], so I'm screwed."

It doesn't have to be that way.

There's nothing wrong with feeling so-called negative emotions. The goal isn't to never feel angry, sad, guilty, or reactive again; the goal is to take responsibility for those emotions. (And if that's triggering to you, please don't stop reading. You will thank me later. Imagine me smiling at you). In fact, grief—for the past, for yourself, for what you never had but wished you did—is completely natural and normal...imperative, even.

Here's the big "but": when you're chronically angry, sad, bitter, disappointed, and reactive, perhaps you don't perceive that you're responsible for those emotions. You believe you either don't have a choice, or that you're being made to feel them—by your mother. You find yourself stuck and unable to move beyond this pain, so you tell these stories over and over again.

It may seem foreign to you right now, but consider that you can have compassion for yourself as you grieve, and as you process all those other emotions. Your mother might not have been able to do this for you or for herself, but it's worth trying and practicing.

Is it sometimes uncomfortable or scary? Yes. Still, there was a time when I saw myself as completely broken, unfixable, and, well, doomed. Doomed to a life of mediocrity. I was wrong. So wrong.

CHAPTER 7
WHAT'S YOUR STORY?

....

Many women have a mother story. A story they use to define themselves, to limit themselves, to react from, to blame from, and to shame themselves from. The funny thing is, these stories—on the surface—don't appear to be about our mothers.

They often look or sound something like this:

"I'm not good enough!"

"I can't have what I want."

"It doesn't matter what I want."

"I don't know what I want."

"I wish someone would just tell me what to do."

"I'm overwhelmed."

"I can't help it."

"I'm so stressed out!"

"I'll take care of myself later."

"Who do I think I am?"

"I can't say no."

"I'm a control freak...that's just the way I am."

"If I don't do it, they'll be mad!"

"She pisses me off!"

"How much more do I have to do?"

None of this is bad news. It doesn't mean you're weak, pathetic, or a loser. It doesn't mean that you're anything short of an amazing, powerful woman right this very minute. It just means that you've got a belief pattern that is looping in your brain: in other words, a story.

That's what this book is about—examining your stories and freeing yourself from them, so you can come home to yourself as an autonomous, resilient woman. You will be accumulating moments of consciousness and allowing yourself to practice concepts that will eventually become part of who you are.

> *Owning our stories and loving ourselves through that process is the bravest thing that we will ever do. —Brené Brown*

I used to think that owning my story meant telling anyone who would listen about all the things my mother did and said to me. When I came across Brené's quote, I wondered why she said it was brave, because I didn't feel brave. I usually felt a combination of vindication and guilt.

I didn't realize what it meant to truly own my story, but once I did, I started to understand what Brené meant when she said it is the bravest thing we'll ever do.

So what is a story? Here's the distinction I like to make: there's what happened (the facts), and then there's what we've made it mean, specifically about us and our mothers. That is the story.

What matters most about our stories is the way in which we tell them and the meaning we derive from them. By our very nature, humans create meaning. Since meaning comes with looking back, we have the opportunity to make meaning that either holds us back or supports our growth. Our stories always have the potential to do both.

Most women have stories they tell about their mothers. Some of the stories are about their childhoods, and others are more recent. Here are some of the stories my clients have told me:

"She abused me."

"She is an alcoholic."

"She was depressed."

"She neglected me."

"She's a narcissist."

"She makes fun of me."

"She slept with my boyfriend."

"She always ruins Thanksgiving."

"She's always late."

And so on.

Here is the way I used to tell my story:

My parents got divorced when I was three, and my mother got remarried to a violent alcoholic. They both drank too much, and they were abusive to me and to each other. I grew up in a chaotic, violent household.

My mother was also very controlling of me and put me on diets, even though I wasn't really overweight. She was jealous of me. And as I got older, it just got worse.

She had no boundaries and because I had no clue who I was (because she controlled me), I just let her continue to run my life. Every time I tried to strike out my own, she either guilted me back into line or threatened or criticized. I never felt like I could make a move without my mother's approval. And when I tried to do something I loved, she'd criticize it.

I started binge eating in middle school. I gained weight. I had a series of bad relationships with men. I have to either hate her or be her doormat. I don't want it to be this way, but I have to protect myself. Basically I have no self-esteem, and my life has sucked because of my mother.

I finally cut her out of my life a few years ago, thinking that everything would be much easier, but it hasn't been. I am wracked with guilt most of the time...and fear too. But a lot of the time I feel white-hot, impotent anger.

You might be thinking, "But Karen, if those things happened, you have a right to be angry! You have a right to feel the way you do." And sure, I was a helpless victim at one point in my life. But my story didn't empower me. My story kept me stuck.

How? Because of the unconscious painful beliefs I had about me as a result. These are some of the painful stories I told myself, about myself:

I am powerless.

I should be ashamed.

I am ashamed.

I have no idea what I want.

She knows what's best.

Being who I am isn't okay.

My body is wrong.

Anything I might want for me is also hers.

I am stupid.

I am irresponsible.

I don't know any better.

I am helpless.

I am pathetic.

I am too much.

I am too big for my britches.

I can never win.

I can't take care of myself.

I can't trust myself.

I can't trust her.

I am bad, silly, or stupid, unless I am doing what she thinks I should do.

I am selfish.

What I feel isn't real.

I don't know what I really feel.

My feelings should be shut down.

That is what I was telling myself, about me. That's what I made all of that other stuff mean.

Here comes the brave part: I did that to myself. I created that story and I hurt myself with it.

It might have been something I naturally learned from my experiences. It might be what was modeled by both my mother and my grandmother. It might have started as something someone who should have loved me was "doing to me."

But I didn't have to internalize all that—or enforce it on myself forever. It wouldn't create the possibility for my life to ever be different, or for all that I truly could become to actualize. When I owned it, when I realized that I had been doing it to myself, I was deeply ashamed. I can feel the prickle of shame on my face even now, just writing about it.

And then? I realized how deeply powerful I am. This is what I call my *woo-hoo-oh-s**t* moment.

It's the moment I *got* (way down deep in my soul...in my cells) that I create the way I experience life with my thoughts and emotions. All of them. The good, the bad, and the ugly: the pain, the joy, the guilt, the shame, the grief, the ecstasy, the love, the sadness.

First came the *woo-hoo!*

I created the joy! I created the pain! I don't have to rely on anyone else! I don't have to blame anyone...even myself! Look how freaking powerful I am! What else might I create? "*Woo-hoo!*"

Then came the "*oh-s**t!*"

Wait, what?! What did I do to myself? And...if I am that powerful, what does that mean? What do I now have to be responsible for?!

Here's the truth: There's no way I could go back to believing that I didn't have the power to create, because what has been seen and felt cannot be unseen and unfelt.

I spent years in therapy (not to mention all the time spent reading those books about mothers who can't love and narcissistic mothers) wallowing around in my sad story, continuing to feel stuck and powerless, believing that—because of my past—I wouldn't be able to change.

This work isn't about digging around in your past and wallowing in sad stories. It's about embarking on a joyful journey from where you are right now. You *get* to do this!

That said, I understand. I get that there are issues from the past—issues concerning your mother—issues that might go all the way back to when you were born, or even before that. I also get that they feel fixed and permanent. We tend to adopt an "I am less-than" persona when we have mother issues, because it keeps us safe in a twisted way. We allow ourselves to be dependent, and we allow others to dictate who we're allowed to be, in order to receive what we believe "love" is (i.e., our mother's approval). It's important to acknowledge and honor those issues and the stories we've told about them ever since.

Something to consider: If you are suffering, the story you are telling yourself isn't "the truth."

Something to journal on: Pick one specific example—concerning your relationship with your mother—that causes you pain. Then...

1. Write down as many details about this example or situation as you can. Don't censor yourself. Write down what your mother did or didn't do; what your mother should have done; what she shouldn't have done; how your life would have been different if it had or hadn't happened. Write it all down. Get the whole thing out of your head.

2. Pare it down to the bare facts, with no opinion or judgment placed on it. It might look like this: My mother said _____.

3. Ask yourself what you made it mean about you and write it down.

4. When you think about what you wrote in step 3, how do you feel?

5. Now list the things you do (or don't do) when you feel that way. In other words, how do you show up in the world when you feel that way?

6. Describe what your life looks like as a result.

7. Sum up your story as briefly as you can. You'll end up with something like this:

8. My mother said _____. I made it mean that I am _____. There's a part of me that feels

_____ because _____. And when

I think about that I feel _____. And when

I feel that way I _____. As a result, I

_____.

Something to practice: Forgive yourself for the things you told yourself about yourself that aren't really true about you. Imagine what it would feel like to let that story go!

From here, you can start to redefine who you are now, as an emotionally adult woman, not as a little girl. What is it that you want for yourself and your life? An important distinction here: don't magnify the "againstness" (emphasizing what you don't want, who you don't want to be) without knowing what it is you do want. With a clear definition of what you want and what you expect for your life, you can begin to create and set boundaries from a place of love for yourself, versus having to react defensively or construct your entire life around avoiding negative experiences.

CHAPTER 8
YOU ARE A COURAGEOUS, CONSCIOUS CREATOR

···

I once worked with a young woman who grew up in a chaotic and abusive family, much like I did. She told me that she'd noticed that chaos and "reaction" felt normal—safe even—and that she was frustrated because she craved healthy routine and peace.

In the moment she recognized this and took a moment to write it down, she stopped reacting and started responding.

She created a moment of awareness. She created a moment of peace.

And then (she said), she bounced back into chaos... and frustration.

This is normal. This is human. When our brains are used to one way of being, and they're introduced to a new way of being, they will tend to bounce back to what they're used to.

For those of us who grow up in chaos, chaos can feel normal and familiar.

With courage, devotion, creativity, and practice, we can transform from being reactionary, frustrated daughters who sometimes find patience and peace...into patient, peaceful women who are—from time to time—reactionary and frustrated.

It's in those reactionary and frustrated moments that we can breathe and place our hands over our hearts, even if just for a moment.

(Consciously create peace for yourself: hands-over-heart is a simple and quick way to calm the amygdala—a.k.a. our "lizard brain"—which is responsible for the fight/flight/freeze reaction.)

Conscious creativity (which takes place in the prefrontal cortex) is the opposite of fear (which takes place in the amygdala).

The more aware you become, the more you recognize that you now have a choice and that you have preferences—you get to create what you would prefer.

Sometimes what you prefer will be at odds with what you unconsciously create. Sometimes you will stumble and feel awkward. Sometimes you won't be able to "out-think" your negative thoughts, and nor should you. This isn't about being "happy-happy-joy-joy" all the damned time. No. That's a recipe for chronic anxiety.

Your power lies in consciousness—in knowing that it doesn't matter whether you create chaos or peace in any given moment.

Your power lies in knowing that you, in fact, created.

You might say to yourself, "But I shouldn't create chaos for myself! I should create peace!"

Rather than beat yourself up for what you have created, revel in the contrast of what's possible.

Something to consider: When you were a child, you didn't have as much of a choice as you do now. What was created for you, and modeled for you, was powerful then, but it's not as powerful as your now-conscious mind.

Something to journal on: What do you want to create? Write—stream-of-consciousness-style—for fifteen minutes about all the things you'd love to create. Nothing is off-limits. You can create things, emotions, states of being, relationships...don't censor yourself.

Something to practice: Pick something from the list and practice creating it. Think of the result, then ask yourself: "What actions do I need to take in order to have that result?" Then ask yourself: "How do I need to feel in order to take that action?" And then ask yourself: "What do I need to believe in order to feel that way?" You are now consciously creating.

CHAPTER 9

BUT WHAT ABOUT THE ANGER/ SADNESS/GRIEF/BITTERNESS/ GUILT I STILL FEEL?

···

> "The essence of trauma is disconnection from ourselves. Trauma is not terrible things that happen from the other side—those are traumatic. But the trauma is that very separation from the body and emotions. So, the real question is: 'How did we get separated and how do we reconnect?' Because that's our true nature—our true nature is to be connected. In fact, if that wasn't our true nature, there would be no human beings. The human species—or any species—could not evolve without being grounded in their bodies." —Dr. Gabor Maté

The only thing feeling anger, sadness, grief, bitterness, guilt—or any of the other myriad emotions you might feel—proves is that you're a normal, functioning human.

There's nothing to fix, turn off, or control. There's nothing wrong with you.

The first exercise may have brought up some intense, uncomfortable, and perhaps unwanted emotions. When those kinds of feelings come up, we tend to be in a hurry to get rid of them. This means we "act" without allowing ourselves to fully feel, express, and most importantly, see what they are trying to teach us.

We have a tendency to think that if we allow ourselves to feel painful emotions, they will never go away and they will overtake us. In fact, the opposite is true. When you can make room for painful emotions, actively accept them, and not be in a hurry to change them, you learn something that you wouldn't have otherwise learned.

So, what are emotions?

Emotions are energy in motion—vibrations in our bodies that we can feel physically—that are usually described in one word. Happy. Sad. Angry. Scared. Happiness has a vibration. Anger has a vibration. Sadness has a vibration. Fear has a vibration.

Emotions are not thoughts or ideas. They are not concepts with long, vague descriptions. They are not opinions or judgments.

The way emotions feel in my body may be different than the way they feel in your body.

Sometimes emotional vibrations are uncomfortable. I've learned that allowing myself to feel an uncomfortable emotion has never, ever hurt me or anyone else. The earth didn't open up and swallow me whole, nor did I explode into a million pieces.

Acting on emotions without consideration is a different story.

And while emotions themselves are not thoughts or ideas, in the vast majority of cases they come from our identity, beliefs, and thoughts. Something happens, and our brains assess what happened and assign meaning to it. That meaning then informs how we feel. All of this happens in an instant, usually without our awareness.

Here's a pertinent example. A few years ago, my mother sent me an email asking a question about my grandmother's trust. I immediately became angry. Seething, even. The reason I became angry wasn't because she sent an email and asked a question. I became angry because of what I made her question mean. I made it mean that I was an incapable, stupid lazy-ass (and we'll get into more details about this email in upcoming chapters).

That's how it works: something happens, we think a thought about it, assign a meaning to it, and voilà—the feeling arises. The more often we repeat these thoughts and feelings, the more automatically this increasingly "hardwired" pathway of emotional processing happens. It becomes a habit for our brains because brains like to be efficient.

How many times have you wondered what it means to feel your feelings? Or to "sit with" them? The reason this can be so confusing or difficult is that we're used to acting on the emotion without fully noticing it.

This is because we were not taught to notice or otherwise pay attention to emotions. In fact, we were pretty much taught the opposite—to ignore, resist, and even distrust them.

But here's the thing: every human being has the capacity and the ability to literally feel every human emotion.

Even the ugly, uncomfortable ones. We're built to feel all of them, so it stands to reason that we're capable of feeling them without harming ourselves. Our bodies are great at feeling emotions, and they are amazingly efficient at it.

Consider the story of Dr. Jill Bolte Taylor, a neurologist who had a stroke. In her book, My Stroke of Insight, she describes that after her stroke, she was unable to resist feeling emotions. Without that ability, but all the while retaining her curiosity about the human mind, she found that for her, an unresisted emotion would last about ninety seconds.

We feel surges of love. Surges of anger. Surges of grief. And then they recede. Even an emotion as intense as grief or anger gives us a break. Sure, they come around again, and as long as we let them flow on through, they will again recede.

But sometimes, because we're afraid to feel a feeling—or because we think certain emotions are bad or wrong—the fear intensifies the already uncomfortable emotion. When we resist anger, we create more anger. We get angry at our anger. We worry about our anxiety. We're disgusted by our hate. We create more pain by telling ourselves we shouldn't be in pain. We don't want to feel that uncomfortable feeling!

And so, because we assign a negative meaning to emotions like anger or jealousy, we tend to spend a lot of time avoiding, stuffing, distracting, and intellectualizing these emotions—so we don't have to feel them—because we consider them ugly and uncomfortable.

Now, consider the difference between resisting an emotion and just letting it vibrate. Imagine that you're about to experience an emotion you find uncomfortable, like panic or terror, but you will only experience it for two minutes. Once the two minutes is up, you're done. What would it be like to just experience it? Without avoidance, resistance, numbing? What might you notice?

This is what I mean when I talk about safely feeling an emotion. And yes, it takes practice, but it's fascinating to experiment with this.

The more you experiment with feeling your feelings, the more you will learn from them. Even better, when you focus on literally feeling the emotion in your body, the faster it goes away! The more you practice noticing and feeling emotions, the easier it gets.

I figure that if your body is capable of feeling all the emotions, then all feelings are valid and worthy of being felt. They're all useful. They all have messages or even lessons for you.

Now let's talk about safely expressing emotions, which includes verbal and non-verbal expression.

It's interesting to watch little children express emotion. Think about an angry or distraught toddler who throws herself to the floor, kicks her legs, and flings her arms. What she is doing is letting her body feel and express the emotion. Or if she's sad, she cries, sobbing and shaking, using her whole body. The same goes for expressing joy with a full-body laugh! Our culture and our families down through the generations have taught us, however, that some emotions are bad—or at least that certain expressions of certain emotions are bad and wrong.

For instance, we teach toddlers that the grocery store floor isn't the best place to express anger. And somewhere along the way, we also learn that some people don't like the way we express certain emotions. If we want attention, love, or approval from them, we quickly learn to stop expressing these emotions, or maybe even feeling them altogether. And sometimes we see someone (our mothers?) expressing an emotion we deem ugly, and we decide we don't want to be like them!

So how do you safely express emotion? Especially, how do you safely express an emotion like anger, which can also feel dangerous? It's important to remember that feeling anger (or other so-called "negative" emotions) does not make you a bad or "un-evolved" person. You are never "above" having feelings. Emotions like anger become a problem if we pick up a knife and stab someone with it because we're angry. Or if we scream at them. It's okay to let it take as long as it needs to take to feel your pain. It's not okay to treat people poorly while you're doing it.

So what does look like in real life? I'll use an example from my own life.

A while back, my husband and I had a minor argument that escalated into raised voices with both of us wanting to be right about something. This is unusual for us. I noticed, pretty much right away, that I had some anger going on. I realized that this anger had nothing to do with the subject. This is why I practice...a lot! It wasn't all that long ago that a situation like this would have derailed me, and I would have felt totally out of control with anger.

Step 1: Notice. Notice the vibration. Focus on how it feels, and let yourself feel it.

Step 2: Next, you want to acknowledge it to yourself. "I'm angry. I'm pissed. I'm frustrated." Continue to feel the vibration. And start moving your body in a way that feels natural.

When I am angry, I like to stomp my feet and pump my arms up and down. In the situation with my husband, I chose to go for a walk with loud, intense music playing on my iPhone, and I pumped my arms and muttered under my breath. There have been other times when I chose to stomp around my basement and yell. And yet other times, when I went outside, threw rocks, and swore.

Cry if you need to cry. Scream if you need to scream. Punch a pillow. Take a walk. Swear out loud if it helps. Throw rocks. Let it take as long as it needs to take. This emotion, or energy in motion, will start to dissipate naturally—and probably pretty quickly, depending on how old it is.

Step 3: Be curious and fascinated about what you just experienced. Ask yourself what message your emotion had for you. As with most intense emotion, the message is usually from the past; the feeling isn't new—it's an old emotion that we've stuffed, and something triggered it. So now we've had an opportunity to heal it.

Step 4: Take responsibility for your emotion. This step may seem counterintuitive; at first, we might think, "Wait, my husband made me angry. He wasn't listening, and he wasn't agreeing with me." But the fact is that my anger is my anger, not his. I'm the one feeling it, and I am the one responsible for the safe expression of it.

Now, that's not to say that I didn't talk to my husband about it later, after I expressed it on my own. I did, but after processing and fully feeling that anger, I was able to speak calmly and without blaming him.

So you're probably thinking, "Wait...I'm supposed to remember all of that the next time I get pissed off?" Nope. It's not all going to happen naturally and automatically, right off the bat. It's a practice, not a perfect. This is something that you become aware of and try out. A little at a time.

The ugly, uncomfortable emotions you experience regarding your relationship with your mother aren't necessarily going to go away. In fact, it is a safe bet they will not go away completely. You can, however, learn to feel and express them safely, without hurting yourself or your mother.

You'll be able to "do" your emotions.

This isn't a book for you to finish reading, put down, and then find everything you're feeling afterwards is simply all "happy-happy-joy-joy." Nothing is further from the truth. Instead, this is a process about allowing yourself to become emotionally fluent by understanding where your feelings are actually coming from and developing ways to manage them safely.

Allowing yourself to feel your feelings all the way through is the ultimate act of re-mothering yourself—of holding the space for yourself in a way that, perhaps, your mother couldn't or wouldn't do.

Something to consider: Avoiding, ignoring, resisting, stuffing, distracting, distrusting, or intellectualizing emotions will make them unconscious and chronic. This is how you hurt yourself (and sometimes others) with your emotions. Complaining, wallowing, and stewing are really just other ways of resisting emotion. It's more profound to acknowledge and feel an emotion, rather than saying "I'm past that."

Something to journal on:

- What are you feeling now?
- How do you know that you are feeling it?
- Where is this feeling in your body?
- What color is this feeling?
- Is this feeling hard or soft?
- Is this feeling fast or slow?
- What else can you say about how this feels?
- How does this feeling make you want to react?
- What judgments do you have about this feeling?
- Why are you feeling this?

- What is the thought or belief that is causing you to have this feeling?

Something to practice: Get to know what various emotions feel like in your body and then notice them. Practice letting them vibrate without doing or saying a thing. Breathe.

Additional journal prompts:

- Think about a time when you believed that your mother caused you to have a negative feeling, then write down what she did or said.

- Describe how she "made" you feel.

- Describe why you think she has the power to create your feelings in this way.

- Describe your feeling without the influence of your mother. (What you would be feeling if she hadn't "made" you feel this way?)

- What is the thought you are thinking that is causing this feeling?

- Make a list of all the emotions you associate with your mother and your relationship with her. For each one, actually take the time to summon up the vibration in your body and describe it. Play with it, and notice how you can increase it and decrease it at will.

One more thing to consider: There are several emotion-like words that are actually not emotions, but rather opinions or interpretations. Here are some of those words (with thanks to Marshall Rosenberg and his book,

Nonviolent Communication: A Language of Life):

abandoned, abused, attacked, betrayed, boxed-in, bullied, cheated, coerced, cornered, diminished, distrusted, interrupted, intimidated, manipulated, misunderstood, neglected, pressured, provoked, put down, rejected, unappreciated, unheard, unseen, unsupported, unwanted, used

These words do not express emotion; they describe thoughts, opinion, and interpretation, which, when you choose them, create emotion. They express how you interpret others, rather than how you feel. This is a crucially important distinction to make, because this is how you start to take back your power!

CHAPTER 10
TRIGGERS AND BUTTONS AND THORNS, OH MY!

One of my favorite lessons of all time comes from Michael Singer, author of *The Untethered Soul*. It goes like this:

There once was a woman who had a thorn in her arm and that thorn directly touched a nerve. Anything that touched the thorn created pain inside her. Even a leaf brushing against it caused pain.

So, even though she loved to take walks in the woods she stopped doing that. She started avoiding the woods, or anything that might touch the thorn.

She built her life around protecting that thorn, believing that's how she would protect herself from pain. What she didn't realize is that she had another option: to remove the damned thorn.

We all have these thorns (or buttons, triggers...whatever you want to call them), and we don't want anybody to touch, push, or pull them. And if someone does, we get all upset, because no one should have touched our thorn. We train people not to touch our thorns, and we build a life around not getting hurt.

"Avoid my thorn." Don't go there with me!

But here's the thing: when we believe that we have triggers, buttons, and thorns, we're giving away all of our power. We're making others responsible for how we feel. The alternative is to understand you can remove that thorn... and if you remove it, you won't have to think about it again.

So how do you know what your thorns are? Disturbance tells you. Annoyance. Frustration. Reaction. In other words, emotion.

Just like pain happens when a physical thorn gets stuck in your skin, disturbance happens when you believe you have a metaphorical thorn. This is why the previous chapter's lesson on understanding emotion—and how to feel and identify what emotion you're experiencing—is so important.

If something touches your thorn—let's say your mother says something—and you notice a disturbance, you can then decide what to do about it. To remove the thorn, confront the feeling and ask yourself: "Do I like being disturbed?" The answer is usually "No." Although it can sometimes be "Yes," and I'll explain why with a personal story later on.

This chapter is about understanding where that disturbance actually comes from, and learning how to be aware.

I've been known to get mightily disturbed when my mother sends me emails. I used to read tone and meaning into everything she wrote. Before I knew better, my "thorn" was telling me: "She's picking a fight with me, she disrespects me, and she thinks I am stupid." Even though I had gotten to the point where I knew better than to react in the moment and fire back, I would still become incredibly angry and/or hurt.

The reason was not because of what she actually wrote in the emails, but rather because of what I made her words mean (e.g., she's picking a fight, she disrespects me, she thinks I am stupid).

Now, of course there's a lot of history here. More than fifty years of it. But what I didn't realize is that I had a very old, unconscious thought that was running the show: she's attacking me—I am her victim, and she is the villain.

That was my thorn. Before I learned this distinction, I often interpreted what my mother said or did as an attack. I spent a lot of time avoiding, fearing, and being angry. Those emotions tended to drive behavior that I am not proud of.

While I would tell anyone who would listen that I was pissed off or hurt, I also liked being angry at my mother. I liked this disturbance because I believed that my anger protected me and my "I am her victim" thorn, just like the woman with an actual thorn in her arm believed that staying out of the woods protected her. Once I understood that, I was able to start removing my thorn.

Your mother may well be deliberately manipulating you and creating frustrating circumstances. She may know your buttons well enough to activate your meltdown sequence. When you recognize that this is what she's doing, you can choose not to allow it to work.

One client said to me, "My mother pushes my buttons so hard that I end up in tears every time I talk to her." And boy, could I relate. I used to think my mother liked being able to make me react; she liked having that kind of power over me. And maybe that was true.

So what do you do when you believe your mother is doing this on purpose? Do you call her on it, or do you just change your reaction? As my client said to me after understanding and practicing this concept:

"My mother tries to keep the upper hand in our dialogue by pushing my emotional buttons until I lose control. My composure and my reaction is my choice. I can practice how to respond in a safe and strong manner when this happens, until it is no longer a predictable pattern for her, or for me."

So how do you start?

Something to practice: Awareness. Start to notice your disturbances and reactions to everything and everyone around you. Take a week to experiment with noticing and observing (especially regarding your interactions with your mother or anyone with whom you feel "reactive").

Instead of engaging in the behaviors of other people, or with every thought you have, just look. Pretend you are there only to observe. When you just look but don't engage, it's interesting how you can release yourself from your own stories about what other people are sharing. How you save more energy for you. How it helps still your mind.

You simply recognize the trigger ("oh look, there it is"), pause, notice what emotions come up, and choose to be fascinated ("how interesting it is that I now feel [insert emotion here] as a result") instead of being frustrated and beating yourself up for having the trigger in the first place.

Of course this doesn't mean you go mute in a conversation. If appropriate, you can say "Oh," or "I see what you mean," or "Oh yes, I hear what you're saying." You can also give body cues by looking at others as they speak, nodding your head "yes" to show you understand, being still (i.e., not multitasking or fidgeting), and giving them your full attention.

When you become the Observer, it's curious how you see people differently. And yourself.

Something to journal on:

- What are you observing?
- Did you notice your thorns, buttons, and triggers?
- What are they?

CHAPTER 11

DEACTIVATE YOUR TRIGGERS, UNBUTTON YOUR BUTTONS, AND PLUCK OUT THOSE THORNS

••

R emember the email from my mother I told you about in Chapter 9? The one she sent in regard to my grandmother's trust?

I am going to use that example to teach this concept. Here—expletives *not* deleted—is what went through my head (and came out of my mouth when I shared with a friend), right after I received that email from her:

So this morning, she sent me an email asking if I have to dip into the principal of my grandmother's trust to keep her at the nursing home, or if there are enough dividends generated by her holdings to pay for her care.

I decided to email my contact at the investment house and ask her to help me answer the question. I wanted to have my facts lined up. I didn't hear back from her today, but had planned on responding to my mother when I got the appropriate answer.

This evening, my mother wrote again and asked if I had an answer—or did I have to check with my husband or my grandmother's lawyer. I was pissed. She thinks I'm an idiot who couldn't possibly figure this out on her own.

Besides...I don't have to jump when she says jump. F**k you, mom. So next, I emailed the lawyer and asked if I am legally obligated to respond to her original question? It's not that I don't want to respond, but I don't want to be manipulated or strong-armed into it.

F**k. I know this is all a big story. And I am still looking for permission outside of myself to tell me that I don't have to keep up this charade with this woman! My f**king mother! Anger. Yes, I am angry! I've been allowing myself anger from time to time (really truly allowing myself to feel it and express it...not to her...no need to do that), but not enough to cut it off for good, because then the guilt takes over and I think I should be evolved enough...I should be able to manage my mind enough...to love her even when she f**king pushes my f**king buttons. And then I beat myself up for having the f*king button in the first place.

I am betting you can relate on some level. Here's how to slow it all down, and start to make sense of all the crap swirling in your head.

But first let me say this: I believe that we all have a unique essence. Some call it a soul. It's what makes us, us. It's the pure core of us. As we live, learn, and grow, we develop identifies and beliefs that inform how we experience and relate to the world outside of us.

Very rarely are we taught, either on purpose or by what our parents and other teachers model, how to consciously create the way we experience and relate to the world.

As I mentioned early on in this book, I have studied and learned from many teachers in the coaching and personal development fields.

Here is how I distill what I've learned:

Circumstances and situations are the things that happen in the world around us that we can't control: the weather, our past, and other people's actions and behavior. Circumstances and situations are factual and neutral, without judgment.

Example: "My mother sent me an email."

Thoughts are the opinions and judgments that constantly run through our minds. Sometimes we're aware of them, but often we aren't. Sometimes we consciously choose thoughts about the circumstances in our lives, but oftentimes our more unconscious beliefs and identity are running the show.

Example: "She's picking a fight with me," "She thinks I'm stupid," "I'm an idiot who couldn't possibly figure this out on my own," and "I don't have to jump when she says jump."

Our conscious and unconscious thoughts create our beliefs and identity.

Beliefs and Identity are the state of mind in which we think something to be the case, based on who we believe ourselves to be, with or without there being empirical evidence to prove that something is the case with factual certainty. We are sometimes unconscious to our beliefs.

Example: If my mother is angry at me, I might die (and yes, this sounds very dramatic, but bear with me). I am her victim (that's the identity piece). I am a pathetic loser.

While our thoughts help us form our beliefs and identity, our beliefs and identity continue to inform how and what we think; how we interpret circumstances and experiences, and how we feel about them. They are the lens through which we view the world. We often think our identities are set in stone and unchangeable.

Emotions (or feelings) are energy in motion—literal vibrations that we experience in our bodies—and they are often related to the thoughts we're thinking, what we believe about ourselves and others, and the identities we've carved out for ourselves (refer back to Chapter 9 for more on emotions).

Example: feeling spitting angry because I believe my mother thinks I'm stupid.

Our emotions often inform how we act and behave.

Actions refer to behavior, reaction, or inaction, and they're often driven by our needs and feelings.

Example: passive/aggressive treatment of my mother, bitching and moaning to my husband, bitching and moaning to my friends, and emailing the lawyer with righteous indignation.

We take action to meet our needs.

Needs are the things all people must have to survive. Common needs include autonomy (being able to choose dreams, goals, and values and plans for fulfilling them), celebration, integrity, interdependence (connection, love, belonging, respect, trust, understanding), physical nurturance (air, food, movement, safety, rest, shelter, touch, water, sexual expression), play, spiritual communion, growth, and contribution. (There are many resources on the subject of human needs. The list of needs I included here comes from Marshall Rosenberg's Nonviolent Communication process.)

When we're aware of and honoring and meeting our needs, our actions reflect it. Our actions also reflect when our needs are not being met. Sometimes needs collide.

Example: My actions (as described above) reflected a misguided attempt to meet my need for integrity and autonomy. And, if I am honest, my perceived need to be right about my mother!

Outcomes and results are the effects of our actions.

Example: I was not in the driver's seat of my own life, because I am choosing to live in reaction to my mother— and having friends who dread my phone calls.

Our outcomes and results provide evidence.

Evidence is the available information indicating whether a belief or proposition is true or valid.

Example: I didn't have an answer for my mother. I had to ask my contact at the bank and my grandmother's lawyer for the answer. See? I *am* pathetic and stupid.

Our outcomes and results tend to provide evidence for, and prove, our thoughts and beliefs. When we believe what we think, we automatically feel and act as if its true, and then we react in ways that get the results that tend to prove us right. This is why our minds can be so tricky. Of course we believe our experiences. But we fail to appreciate that it was not the only possible outcome.

Taking the time to slow it all down and see each component helps us become much more aware of the impact each component has on our lives. From there we can become more intentional with how we create our lives.

Something to consider: We might not be able to change our circumstances, but we can question and interrupt our beliefs, identity, thoughts, and patterns. Here are some powerful pattern-interrupting questions:

"Who am I when I _____?" (Identity)

"Who do I want to be when I _____?" (Identity)

"What am I making that circumstance mean?" (Thoughts)

"Why am I choosing to think this way right now?" (Beliefs)

"Am I acting from the belief that I am safe or that I am in danger?" (Actions & Beliefs)

"What happens when I respond this way instead of that way?" (Results)

"What need am I trying to meet?" (Needs)

"What need might she be trying to meet? (Needs)

"What does this outcome seem to prove?" (Evidence)

Something to journal on: Choose a recent interaction with your mother and break it down as I did in the example above. It doesn't matter where you start. Sometimes it's easier to notice how you feel and put that down first. The components I described above, in the order in which I used them, are:

- Circumstances (keep it neutral...just the facts);

- Thoughts (the sentences that run through your mind...opinions, judgments, stories);

- Beliefs/Identity (your general state of mind and who you believe yourself to be);

- Emotions (one word to describe a vibration in your body);

- Actions (behavior, inaction, reaction, how you show up, which are often driven by needs and emotions);

- Needs (what you must have to survive, as well as things that improve quality of life);

- Outcome/Results (the effects of actions, behavior, inaction, reaction); and

- Evidence (the information that indicates to you that your beliefs and thoughts are true).

Something else to consider: This isn't about (immediately) changing your thoughts, beliefs, and identity—or trying to be someone you are not. Rather, it's about being conscious and aware. When you see the connection, it may be tempting to want to change your thoughts (i.e., "positive affirmations") so that you can feel better. This can backfire when it doesn't seem to work, especially with beliefs that seem to be deeply entrenched, or an identity that you may think is just part of your makeup. Thoughts like:

- I'm not good enough.
- Who do I think I am?

- I can't take care of myself.

- I am unloveable.

- I have to do it all.

- I'm too big for my britches.

- I don't deserve to have what I want.

- I'm unworthy.

There's an interesting connection between the desire to stop thinking negative thoughts and the ability to stop thinking negative thoughts. Here's how it works. You notice yourself feeling like crap and you realize there must be a negative thought rolling around in your brain. If you're anything like me, you see the pattern. Then you go into "change-that-thought" mode.

But "changing your thoughts" reactively like this is really just another form of resistance, judgment, and avoidance because underneath those negative thoughts are other thoughts like "I shouldn't think that," or "It's so deeply entrenched," or "*Ugh*, I hate that I have these negative thoughts."

We judge those thoughts and thus ourselves, as "bad." The only truth about consistent, pernicious thoughts is that our brains have gotten really good at thinking them. That's it. Our brains love to be efficient and they don't care if those thoughts hurt us. That doesn't make us bad, it actually means our brains are working as intended!

It is possible to change thoughts and beliefs and to let go of identities that no longer serve us, and the first step is awareness. It then becomes a practice. Rather than trying to force it, be kind to yourself and let the process happen naturally and organically.

So, let me say that again: The only reason you continue to think a negative thought is because your brain has gotten good at it. And that's so good to know, because it also means that your brain can get good at thinking other, more helpful thoughts, just as easily. That thought itself is helpful in dispelling the notion that some thoughts are more deeply entrenched than others, which tends to send the message that they're going to be harder to get rid of.

So rather than resisting, trying to change, judging, or pushing away the thoughts that don't feel good, just notice them. Watch when those unwelcome thoughts show up, rather than beating yourself up for having them.

CHAPTER 12
A QUICK NOTE ABOUT OUR LITTLE-GIRL BRAINS

....

Dear Karen,

Why am I so afraid of my mother being disappointed in me?

Signed, —many women I've met

* * *

This question is near and dear to my own fearful little-girl heart.

Here's the short answer: we are afraid of our mothers being disappointed in us because in the ancient part of our little-girl brains we (unconsciously) believe that if she's disappointed in us, we will die.

A couple of years ago I uncovered a long-held unconscious belief: "My mother has the power to destroy me. And if she can destroy me, then anyone can."

Thought: I can be destroyed

Emotion: terror

Action: none; or changing and bending and contorting to prevent destruction

The older I get and the more people I talk to, the more I know that pretty much everyone has some version of this thought. I've spent a lot of my life reacting to this thought and/or trying to resist or push the terror away.

Once I became aware of how this thought-emotion-behavior pattern was showing up all over my life I decided to just let it be there. And slowly, over the course of a couple of months, the fear started to melt away...and the belief that I can be destroyed started to wither and die. What once was etched in stone is now ghostly...sort of like something written on an Etch-a-Sketch and then shaken off.

So it's important to understand how our brains work, because you are so not alone when it comes to your fears. I am not a brain expert, so I consulted with Dr. Google and a colleague (Lana Bastianutti) who has a degree in psychology, among other qualifications.

There are three parts of the brain that are pertinent to this discussion: the amygdala (a.k.a. the ancient "lizard" brain), the hippocampus (a.k.a. the "mammalian" brain), and the prefrontal cortex (a.k.a. the "human" brain).

I love this description from the *Know Your Brain—Armed with Science* website: "The amygdala is the stress evaluator. It continuously monitors all situations for danger and decides when to react. The sights, sounds and smells of frightening and dangerous memories are stored there. When the brain recognizes similar situations, the amygdala sends out danger signals and gets the body ready for a flight-or-fight response." It is associated with reactive and reflexive action, and it avoids hazards.

And as I said above, it is that ancient part of our brains that made Mommy to love us because if she doesn't love us, if she's disappointed, our very lives might be at risk. She may decide she doesn't want to feed and care for us anymore.

So even though we're full-grown adults in charge of our own lives, that pesky amygdala has us being vigilant regarding our mothers' approval, validation, and love.

Lana says, "Problems arise when we think that the amygdala (1) represents who we *are*; (2) dictates what we must do; and (3) is in charge. We think that we have no choice. None of that is true."

The hippocampus is involved in the storage of long-term memory, which includes all past knowledge and experiences. It's how we are able, for example, to brush our teeth without really thinking about it. If it were part of a computer, it would be the hard drive. It is also part of the limbic system, which regulates emotion.

Then there's the prefrontal cortex, which is the large part of the brain sitting right behind your forehead. This is the executive-functioning area responsible for rational thought problem-solving, and decision-making. In the computer analogy, this is the central processing unit running the programs. It is all about abstract thought, language, empathy, cooperation, and social cognition.

Lana continues: "Within the higher brain resides the capacity to discern and decide, reason and rationalize, all of which lays the foundation for choice and responsibility. At this level, we have the ability to override anything that the lower brain suggests simply by activating our higher brain functioning. Most of us don't know this. Most of us walk around blindly listening to our lizard brain as it chatters away directing us to seek relief for our discomfort, unaware of the havoc it creates in its wake. We've unwittingly left little room for our higher brain to kick in and kick out the potentially destructive thoughts and habits encouraged by our lower brain."

"More importantly," she adds, "we've left little room for ur true selves to be revealed. Who we really are resides beyond thought. Who we really are remains constant the whole of our lives. Who we really are remains unaffected by thought and belief and memory and habit and opinion and preference and experience. Who we really are, at our highest level, radiates a love and compassion, wisdom and common sense that is utterly devoid of color or creed or religion or gender or orientation. Who we really are lives within all of us."

Don't be afraid of fear. Just notice it.

CHAPTER 13

DO NO HARM, BUT TAKE NO BULL: HOW TO ESTABLISH, ARTICULATE AND MAINTAIN IMPECCABLE BOUNDARIES

••

Most women I work with believe that as long as they are not actively engaged with their mother, they are okay. It's only when they have to interact with her that they find themselves reacting, seemingly not able to "control" themselves.

I like to use the Superman analogy: We are powerful agents in our own lives, and our mothers are Kryptonite. When we're around them, they seem to steal our power!

So the question becomes: Who do you want to be—not only in your relationship to your mother—but in your life? How do you want to feel? How do you want to show up? Do you like and respect who you are most of the time?

On some level, you know your mother isn't going to change (or maybe she will, but you can't count on it), yet you act as if she will. What might happen if you focused on what you can change?

Something magical happens when you decide to respond differently to your mother. You begin to develop self trust, which grows into equanimity, and ultimately Matriarch Mare status. You trust yourself to have your own back and with that comes peace. Sometimes, just loosening your grip on the story of your relationship with your mother leaves room for her to change her patterns, too, but right now we're still focusing on you.

I was afraid to set boundaries with my mother for more than forty years. It's probably more accurate to say that I didn't realize I needed to set boundaries with her until I was about forty, and then I was afraid to do it.

It came down to one simple (mostly unconscious) belief: if I express and stand up for my values, preference, desires (which is basically what boundaries are), then she will reject me. I was afraid to stand up for myself and for what I needed and wanted, because I didn't know how to handle her not approving or validating me. I was afraid she'd criticize me for needing what I said I needed, and for wanting what I said I wanted.

Because of my fear, I engaged in dysfunctional behavior and sometimes tolerated or even perpetuated outright abuse. Not just with my mother, but in other relationships as well. Not to mention how I treated myself. I spent a lot of time angry, reactive, and defensive.

As I mentioned earlier, things came to an ugly head at the end of 2010. She sent me an email that I deemed beyond hurtful. Rather than fighting back, trying to defend or explain myself, I told her never to call or email me again. I was done.

I thought I had set a boundary, but rather than easing my angry, reactive, and defensive feelings, after taking this step I found myself angrier and more defensive, with guilt and deep sadness thrown in for good measure. I spent a lot of time focused on all the ways she'd done me wrong to help me feel better about cutting her out of my life.

In reality, I was out of integrity with myself. Since then, I've been working towards what is sometimes referred to as "radical" self-responsibility: this goes beyond "adulting" and is all about being responsible for my internal world and experience. A big part of that has meant learning how to set healthy boundaries.

A lot of times, before we learn how to have healthy boundaries, we believe our mothers treat us the way they do "because we let them." We think we are supposed to be able to control the way they treat us (probably because that's what's been modeled: our mothers tried to control us in the same way). We contort ourselves trying every conceivable thing in an effort to change, fix, or curtail the challenging aspects of the relationship.

Or maybe someone else suggests that the way our mothers behave is because of something we are not doing, or doing wrong (our culture is quick to guilt daughters...and mothers, for that matter).

If you've been in therapy, it's probably been suggested to you that you learn how to set boundaries, which is a logical next step when you notice that you can't control the way your mother treats you.

Many of us (and in many cases our mothers) believe that boundaries are about other people's behavior—that they are designed to make other people do what we want them to do (or stop doing what we don't want them to do). This is not a boundary, it's an ultimatum.

Here's the distinction I like to make:

A boundary is a request that you make of someone who is infringing on your emotional or physical space in an effort (generally) to improve the relationship. Boundaries are about taking care of (and responsibility for) yourself and often include phrases like "I'd prefer," "I'd value," and "My preferences are...."

An ultimatum is an uncompromising demand you make, the rejection of which often results in the breakdown or end of a relationship ("Do it or else!"). Ultimatums are about controlling the other person (because we think we'll feel better) and often include words like "You should/should not...," "You have to...," or "You can't...."

We find ourselves issuing ultimatums when there are no boundaries in place.

Many of us were taught (not directly, but rather by what was modeled in our families) that ultimatums are boundaries and vice versa. This why we often feel conflicted or mean or bitchy or nasty or selfish when we think about setting boundaries and it's why we might experience backlash after the fact. It's why so many women struggle with this crucial life skill. It wasn't taught or modeled in a loving or realistic way.

Setting boundaries with our mothers is only one part of the equation, because sometimes our mothers will flatly refuse to respect them, So getting clear about our own behavior commits us to something other than destructive reactions as a next step. Knowing we are in integrity with ourselves and with our mothers means we are truly keeping our word to ourselves.

Impeccable boundaries are not:

- mean, rude, or selfish;
- disrespectful;
- orders;
- designed to control, manipulate, coerce, or threaten others;
- meant to change someone else's behavior;
- ultimatums;
- reactive; or
- weapons we deploy.

Impeccable boundaries are:

- healthy;
- respectful;
- about your own behavior;
- a delineation of where you end and others start;
- a tool that promotes self-responsibility;
- a gift you give to others and to yourself;

- a meaningful way for you to take care of and protect yourself;

- based on your values; and

- responsive.

Here are two effective ways to set impeccable boundaries.

(1) Request–Consequence:

The *Request* is what you ask your mother to stop doing whatever it is that crosses your boundary.

The *Consequence* is that you let her know what you will do if she chooses not to abide by or comply with your request. It is an action that you will take. The more well-defined the action, the better and more effective your boundary will be.

Here are some examples:

Request: Please stop yelling at me.

Consequence: If you don't stop yelling, I am going to leave.

Request: The best way to reach me is via email.

Consequence: If you text me or send me messages on Facebook, I won't respond.

Request: I'd love to chat with you once a week for half an hour.

Consequence: If you call me more than that, I won't answer the phone.

Notice that when you make the request, the result is the
action that you will take.

(2) Request–Benefit:

The *Request* is what you ask your mother to stop doing
whatever it is that infringes on your boundary.

The *Benefit* is that you let her know how stopping this
behavior this will improve your relationship.

Here are some examples:

Request: Please stop yelling at me.

Benefit: If you stop yelling, I'll be able to better concentrate
on what you're trying to tell me.

Request: The best way to reach me is via email.

Benefit: If you email, it's easier for me to keep track of
our communication.

Request: I'd love to chat with you once a week for half
an hour.

Benefit: This way I'll be able to give you my
undivided attention.

In either case, it's best to make requests specific and clear
and to let your mother know the impact this will have on
you or on the situation.

The most common boundary-setting mistake you can
make is not following through and/or believing that once

you establish and articulate a boundary, your mother will (or should) respect and honor it.

It's not your mother's job or responsibility to respect your boundaries...it's yours. And this is good news because this is how you begin to take yourself seriously, to keep promises you make to yourself, and show yourself that you are worthy of having boundaries.

It bears mention that your mother most likely didn't teach you to set healthy boundaries, so it stands to reason that she was never taught to employ or respect them. And just as it isn't your fault this wasn't taught, it isn't her fault she doesn't know what she didn't experience.

Setting good, healthy boundaries with my mother was one of the hardest things I've ever done, especially given that there were forty-plus years of a pattern in place: no boundaries. But it was also one of the most liberating things I've ever done. I was finally being honest. I was finally in integrity with myself—and with her.

Let me tell you what's amazing about that. I now rarely have any resentment, bitterness, or anger when it comes to my mother. Because I have honored my boundaries, rather than feeling resentful, bitter, or angry, I feel love.

Here's an example. My mother smokes. She especially likes to smoke when she's in the car (whether she's driving or someone else is). I prefer not to be exposed to smoke. We used to have quite the passive-aggressive drama around it. I'd seethe with anger and say something like, "Can't you wait?!" I would open all the windows and she would close them. I made it mean that she disrespected me and even wanted to harm my health. She made it mean that I was critical of her and was trying to control her.

I finally decided to try setting a boundary around this when she asked me to drive her somewhere. The day before, I made my request: "Mom, I would appreciate it if you didn't smoke in my car. If you'd like to smoke, I will pull over so you can get out and do just that." She agreed. Another time, when she was the one driving, I suggested: "Mom, if you want to smoke in the car, that's fine, I'll drive separately in my own car."

Notice how my language permitted her to continue to smoke, and I didn't have to get angry or upset or make it mean anything. I didn't try to control her behavior, I just controlled mine. Having good healthy boundaries prevents us from having to accept the consequences of someone else's behavior because we're managing our own instead.

Values-based boundary setting promotes self-kindness, self-care, and self-responsibility. It puts you back in the driver's seat of your own life, and allows you to reclaim the power you've been giving to your mother. It helps you love and accept her for who she is, allowing her to behave exactly as she wants to, while taking care of yourself by honoring your needs.

Many women don't want to set boundaries with their mothers because they believe they will risk losing the relationship, or they're afraid their mothers will say "no" and will continue to infringe on their personal and emotional space. (That was me for a very long time). They're afraid that if they take care of themselves and tell the truth, they might make their mothers angry (and then not be able to handle it). So in order to not risk this, they don't set boundaries and they stay in a relationship that is based on lies and resentment.

My Best Boundary-Setting Tips

1. Decide that you love, honor, and value yourself enough to establish boundaries and that you love, honor, and value others enough to teach them how to be with you.

2. Be clear about what you value, knowing that your boundaries will be those values—*in action* (thank you Randi Buckley for this distinction). Some of the values I've identified are respect, curiosity, creativity, humor, intensity, authenticity, trust, discernment, and equanimity. When you are connected to your values in this way, your boundaries will feel like a more natural extension of who you are.

3. Be compassionate. You are modeling an important skill for effective communication. Being compassionate and setting boundaries go together.

4. If you're frustrated, angry, or resentful, you're not ready to set a boundary. Work through those emotions first. Journal (or talk with someone who won't continue to validate your anger) until you can get to a space of calm. The reason you are upset is not because of what the other person is doing (or not doing), it's because you don't have proper boundaries in place and you haven't been speaking your truth.

5. Once you're clean and clear (which basically means that you've taken responsibility for your upset), you can have a

boundary conversation if you want to.

6. It's not necessary to communicate your boundary until someone has violated it. And even then, you don't necessarily have to communicate it, but in order to be effective, you do have to follow through with the action you promised yourself you would take.

7. If you choose to have a boundary conversation, use a neutral tone of voice. If there is a negative (or falsely positive) charge to your communication, then the message can get lost and the clarity of the boundary becomes clouded. Practice speaking without a charge in your voice so it feels natural.

8. Remember that you are not trying to control the other person's behavior. You are changing or adjusting your own behavior in response.

9. Practice your new skill with someone who will offer little resistance. Get a feel for what it is like to make the request. When you get more confident you can start setting boundaries with people who are more challenging.

10. Be responsible for your own communication, but understand that you are not responsible for how the other person receives or interprets it, nor for how they feel as a result. Create clear direct ways of communicating and allow the other person to feel how they choose.

11. Don't take it personally if the other person doesn't change or respect your boundary. Be ready, willing, and able to follow through a change in your own behavior.

12. Practice Non-Defensive Communication (à la Marshall Rosenberg).

Defensive reactions, which, when we use them, keep us in conflict, and the other person in the upper-hand position:

- I am not...
- No I didn't...
- How can you say that...
- Why do you always...
- That's crazy...
- I never did/said...
- I only did it because...
- I didn't mean to...
- I was just trying to...

Non-defensive responses, which defuse the situation and allow us to take the high road (practice using these...some will feel better than others):

- I see.
- I understand.
- That's interesting.
- That's your choice.
- I'm sure you see it that way.
- You're entitled to your opinion.
- I'm sorry you're upset.
- This subject is off-limits.

- I choose not to have this conversation.
- [Fill in the blank] isn't going to work for me.
- I know you're upset.
- This is non-negotiable.

Something to consider: When it comes to boundaries with your mother (or anyone, for that matter), your job isn't to get her behave differently. Your job is to take care of yourself. In deciding what taking care of yourself looks like, you can then make a decision about what your behavior will look like.

Something to journal on: What is the boundary you'd like to set with your mother? What is your intention in setting this boundary? What value can you put into action in support of this boundary? What does taking care of yourself look like? What do you hope to accomplish? What do want the result to be? The benefit? What is your truth? What do you need to take responsibility for?

Something to practice: Briefly and clearly state your boundary using the Request–Consequence or Request–Benefit model. Say it to yourself. Say it out loud. Say it out loud while looking at yourself in the mirror. Say it out loud to someone else and see how it lands.

CHAPTER 14
BOUNDARIES WITH MYSE-HELF

....

(Who gets the early '80s rock reference?)

An experience that stands out clearly in my memory is the time my mother confronted me about something (via email) and I noticed—in the moment—that I was donning my metaphorical boxing gloves to engage in the conflict.

I started typing my angry defense and then something came over me. Another realization. I didn't want to spar.

So I deleted what I had written and wrote instead, "I understand."

She wrote back and thanked me.

The conflict was over.

And I felt amazing.

All I did was acknowledge her. I didn't change or fix the thing about which she was angry.

So what does this have to do with boundaries?

> *Boundaries are your values in action. —Randi Buckley*

I value peace. All those times in the past, when I donned my metaphorical boxing gloves, I was ignoring what I value. And it's my impression that, for whatever reason, my mother doesn't value peace as much as I do.

In fact, I used to think I was weak and ineffective because I either didn't know how—or didn't want—to spar with her. And *that* actually reminds me of the time I hyperventilated during an actual sparring match in a kickboxing class I took years ago.

The way that I can put this value into action is by making an intentional choice to abstain from sparring and to know that I can make an intentional choice to respond in a way that feels right and good to me, which is different than reacting in the moment.

Something to consider: Sometimes, the best way to have boundaries with your mother is to have boundaries with yourself. And the best way to do that is to ask yourself what you value.

Something to journal on: What do you value? How can you inject that value into your relationship with your mother? What can you take responsibility for?

Something to practice: Just notice. Notice, like I did, in the moment that you are reacting to what she's doing or saying, and then observe what's happening in your brain. You are fascinating and you deserve your own compassionate curiosity.

Something else to practice: (This one comes directly from Randi Buckley's Healthy Boundaries for Kind

People.) Imagine you can create a semipermeable bubble around you and that you can fill it with whatever you like: kindness, creativity, respect, grace, humor, etc. Now imagine feeling those traits/values/emotions around you. Remember that it is semipermeable. Some things can come in and others can't. Only the things that can match the energy of what you are holding in your bubble can make it through. Other things will have to gently bounce off and can't get near you. Play with this. Monitor your bubble. Notice. Make choices. *You* choose what makes it through.

CHAPTER 15

"BUT SHE MANIPULATES ME INTO NOT HAVING—OR IGNORING—MY BOUNDARIES"

∙∙

Does your mother manipulate you?

Like I even have to ask, right?

Seriously though...here's what I've figured out about manipulation: we tend to do it when we think there's no alternative to getting what we want and need (remember needs in Chapter 11?).

And our mothers? They were most likely taught that their wants and needs didn't matter. They were taught that women weren't allowed to have wants and needs. And you know what? Acknowledging and honoring our needs and wants go hand-in-hand with impeccable boundaries.

So of course our mothers manipulate and guilt us (and so do we...well, I do, from time to time).

This may be why her boundaries are weak or nonexistent, and it may be why it's so hard for you to establish the boundaries you desire.

Now, here comes a little bit of a mind-bender: your boundaries will become clearer and easier to set, articulate, and maintain when you pay attention—and speak—to your mother's needs (*which does not mean being responsible for meeting her needs!*).

What "needs" am I talking about? Every human on Earth has needs, and pretty much every action any human being takes is an attempt to meet a need (from Chapter 11).

Sometimes we don't like the way our mothers act when they are trying to get their needs met, and we tend to label those actions and behaviors.

Here's a real-life example from a client: "My mother shows off to her friends on Facebook by posting sickeningly sweet 'I love my daughter' memes designed to make her look like an amazing mother...she's such a narcissist."

She might very well be showing off and she may have narcissistic tendencies. But what if this behavior is her way of trying to feel like she belongs, or is relevant? Now I get it...the way she's going about it might be super annoying and/or passive-aggressive, but now you have a needs-related explanation.

So when it comes to her manipulation, look at what needs to be heard, seen, or acknowledged in her. And then check what needs to be heard, seen, or acknowledged in you.

Looking for and speaking to your mother's needs isn't about transforming or contorting or changing yourself to meet them...it's about understanding them so you can set boundaries that are more likely to be effective *and* will help you not feel guilty or mean before, during, or after. In fact, you will probably like and respect yourself in the process. That's a safe destination, and an important one

Something to consider: Everything your mother does (and everything you do) is an attempt to meet a need.

Something to journal on: What need is your mother trying to meet when she manipulates you? When taking a stand for yourself, how can you speak to that need? Knowing the answer to these questions will help you set boundaries in a way that feels good to you.

Something to practice: Look for needs. When you see someone acting a certain way, ask yourself, "What need are they trying to meet?" In this way you will increase your "needs" radar and this will, in turn, help you set better boundaries.

CHAPTER 16

GUILT, ANXIETY, AND FEAR ARE NOT INEVITABLE WHEN IT COMES TO SETTING BOUNDARIES

••

Guess the answer to this question:

"What are the top three emotions you experience when you think about setting boundaries with your mother?"

Guilt, anxiety, and fear. By far. And the question I get asked the most goes something like this:

* * *

Dear Karen,

My narcissistic mother, who has been abusive towards me all of my life, has finally crossed the line. Actually, she's crossed the line many times, but I lacked the courage to do anything about it. Last Thanksgiving she said some unforgivable, unimaginable, disgusting things. Things I will never repeat, but never forget. So began our quasi-estranged relationship.

My mother is alone. She's divorced and in a bad way financially. This past year I didn't invite her to any of my holiday gatherings. My only brother believes I'm a drama queen and doesn't support my decisions regarding our mother.

Meanwhile she continues to try and guilt me via texts and voicemail, hinting that she needs money.

I don't want her at my house. But I feel guilty that if I don't invite her, she will spend holidays alone. I feel like I can't win either way. Without her I feel guilty, with her I feel like I have betrayed myself and supported her ugly behavior. It's a no-win situation.

How the heck does one set boundaries with someone who is so helpless/hopeless?

My response:

I so get this one. It feels like an intractable situation. I spent many years bouncing between guilt (and shame), anger, and hopelessness regarding my relationship with my mother. There was so much drama, and because I was "in" it with her, I couldn't see it.

Guilt, shame, and hopelessness are the reason we don't/ can't/won't set boundaries with our mothers.

That, along with a misunderstanding of what boundaries actually are.

Simply put, boundaries demonstrate what you stand for: your values, your preferences, your needs, and your desires.

If you are not sure what you stand for—or if you don't think you're allowed to have your own values, preferences, needs, and desires—you will feel guilt when trying to establish or assert boundaries.

I love this riff on guilt and boundaries, from Randi Buckley:

Guilt is a sneaky devil.

Guilt keeps you from believing that you deserve to have boundaries

Guilt makes you regret setting boundaries, or even prevents you from doing so.

Guilt prevents you from believing in yourself or from following through.

Guilt arises when you try to manage your mother's response to your boundaries.

Guilt arises when you believe your mother is disappointed with you.

Guilt arises when you believe you're responsible for your mother not agreeing with you.

Guilt arises when you believe that you don't deserve to say "No" or to have boundaries.

Guilt arises when you're not sure if she'll accept or honor your boundaries.

Guilt arises when you're not sure how to express your boundaries.

Guilt arises when you set boundaries in a way that is not in alignment with who you are or does not honor your values.

Something to consider: Oftentimes, the reason we want to have a boundary is because we know it will be good for us. But we're afraid because we think our mothers won't see it as good. There is no such thing as "private" good…what's good for you will serve a greater good.

Something to journal on: What do you want your boundaries to do for you? What do you really want to say? Is there a greater good? What is it? How do you want to establish this boundary? When you imagine putting your values into action, what feels good? What do you want to have happen as a result of this boundary? How do you want things to be with your mother? What do you want your relationship to feel like?

Something to practice: Envision the outcome. Imagine that you've set the boundary and it is being respected, by both you and your mother. What do you see? Feel? Hear?

This practice leaves very little room for guilt and will help you set impeccable boundaries with your mother. And it is very much a practice. Choose to have a beginner's mind… to be a curious, devoted student of your lovely self.

CHAPTER 17
BUT MOTHERS AREN'T
SUPPOSED TO...

One year, just prior to Mother's Day, I saw one of those "things you should never say to..."-type articles. It was entitled "13 Things No Estranged Child Needs To Hear On Mother's Day." Of course I read it.

From the list, here's item #9: "Some people don't even have mothers! You'll regret this when she's gone."

I chose this specific article because of the subject, and because it points to a common theme that plays out between mothers and daughters, not to mention other relationships. Our (mostly unconscious) desire to remain in the victim role is rewarded by implying that others shouldn't say certain things to us.

"Don't say these things to me because I might feel bad or mad or sad."

I get it. Sometimes people (including our mothers) say insensitive, mean, rude, annoying, offensive, or thoughtless things. Sometimes they don't know the whole story. Sometimes it's on purpose and sometimes it's just their own unconscious patterns.

But what if instead of creating rules for others in regard to what they can or can't say to us, we just let them be who they are and say what they want to say? What if, instead of being offended or outraged, we changed or managed our own thoughts and behavior—rather than scolding, should-ing, or "educating" them?

When I'm honoring my inner Matriarch Mare, I am not triggered by what other people say (even my mother!). I am responsible for myself. Managing my response means I get to choose to ignore what my mother said, change the subject, or even walk away. She gets to continue saying whatever she wants to say, or doing whatever she wants to do.

I got this concept on a whole new level several years ago when I told a mentor, "My mother stabbed me in the heart with that email," and she said to me, "You stabbed yourself in the heart with what you made her email mean." I retorted, "But mothers aren't supposed to give their daughters knives with which to stab themselves in the heart!"

Her reply? "Why not?"

Her question might seem a bit harsh, but it brings up a good point: As Byron Katie says, when we argue with what happened by saying it shouldn't have happened that way, we create pain for ourselves. Now I know better, but back then I was *so* attached to my story and to my role as my mother's victim that I couldn't see it any other way.

The point isn't to become a robot who is automatically and immediately immune to what your mother does or says. It's about learning to notice the disturbance and to then ask yourself: "What's really going on here? What am I making it mean?"

It's also about understanding that we can grieve the considerate, nurturing relationship we wish we had. It's not wrong that I felt hurt, but letting that hurt drive my life was definitely a problem for me. Those in the self-help world tend to say things like "don't take it personally" and "it has nothing to do with you and everything to do with the other person." We can logically know that, but when we still feel hurt, it becomes one more thing to beat ourselves up for.

We have shoulds and shouldn'ts all over our lives, not just for ourselves, but for everyone else, including (especially?) our mothers. And why not? Your mother most likely has a whole list of shoulds and shouldn'ts for you, too.

One of the most powerful exercises I ever did, when I decided it was time to go deep in regard to my mother issues, was to make a list of all the things I thought my mother should or shouldn't do (or say), and then acknowledge that the reason I wanted her to change is because of how I thought I would feel. In a word: happier.

Most of the women I work with believe they would happier if their mothers changed or behaved differently. I have come to understand that what my mother says or does has no impact on me emotionally until I think about it, interpret it, and choose to make it mean something. I was really good at making what she said and did mean something bad, which in turn made me sad and angry.

I believed that if she just said and did what I wanted her to, then I could be happy. And I'll tell you something right now. All the shoulds and shouldn'ts I had for my mother guaranteed only one thing: more emotional pain. Having these conditions put my emotions in my mother's hands, and if she didn't abide by my list, I was guaranteed to feel negative emotions. Then I blamed her because I felt bad.

Because I gave control of my emotions to my mother, I perpetuated my hidden belief that I am powerless and that I couldn't take care of myself. When I finally took responsibility for my emotions, I got to feel and experience what I wanted on my own terms, no matter what she did or didn't do (or say). And yes, there are times when I still feel hurt, but I am able to compassionately hold myself accountable for it.

This doesn't mean it's bad to want your mother to do certain things, or to ask her for something you want. Just understand that you will create pain for yourself if you expect her to meet your needs or make you feel good. That's your job.

We tend to feel frustrated when our needs/desires/ preferences go unmet, but frustration isn't a given. We don't *have* to feel frustrated. One solution is to get curious and to let observation transcend your expectation (I'm saying it again: there's nothing wrong with having and communicating expectations).

It's also equally important to remember that you are not responsible for your mother's emotions and unmet needs, and that she is in charge of how she interprets your behaviors. When you let her off the hook for how you feel, you also will give yourself permission to let yourself off the hook for how she feels.

Something to consider: Can you see how having an unwritten list of shoulds and shouldn'ts for your mother is different from having healthy boundaries?

Something to journal on: Write, in detail, what you think your mother should do...what you'd like her to do. For each item, write down why you want her to behave this way.

How would you feel differently if she behaved this way? How would your thoughts about her change if she behaved in this way? Do you want her to behave this way even if she doesn't want to? Why or why not? What do you make it mean that she doesn't behave this way? When she wants you to behave a certain way so she can feel good, what is that like for you? In what other ways has she made you responsible for her feelings?

How might you let yourself off the hook for her feelings? And how might you do the same for her?

Something to practice: Notice, in your day-to-day interactions, when you find yourself thinking about what other people should and shouldn't do or say, not to mention when you "should" on yourself.

CHAPTER 18
THE MYTH OF THE
UNLOVED DAUGHTER

....

One day not all that long ago, a friend tagged me in a thread on Facebook in which an article was shared about why unloved daughters struggle to escape shame. Several women commented that this had been (and in some cases still is) their experience.

"This is my personal story. I wish I had a mother that loved me. I've always been to blame. It's a sad reality."

Several others sort of tsk-tsked about how sad it must be. A pall fell over the conversation.

Given my work, it's not surprising that I hear things like this:

"My mother doesn't love me."

"My daughter hates me."

"My mother has told me she wishes she didn't have kids and wonders what her life would have been like if she didn't have me."

"I don't understand what I did wrong."

"My mother told me she thinks her life would have been so much better if she hadn't had children. It feels like she's saying she wishes I was dead."

I've heard these words from my very own mother in regard to *her* mother.

The pain and suffering are palpable. And understandable.

Something bothered me about that Facebook conversation, though...the idea that it's a "sad reality" if a mother can't or won't love her daughter. As if it's etched in stone and, as a result, the daughter's capacity for joy will remain stunted for the rest of her life.

She becomes someone who is pitied. Someone whose potential is tainted.

Don't get me wrong: I know the pain of thinking my mother doesn't love me. I know what it's like to grow up in an environment saturated in shame. I know what it feels like when I believe my mother is rejecting me. I know that PTSD from growing up with Adverse Childhood Experiences is real.

I also know the oddly satisfying feeling of being pitied and of not living into my potential.

And finally? I know—deep in my bones and in my cells—that I have an infinite capacity for joy and that my potential is equally as infinite. And while I will always make room in my life for sadness and grief, my life is far from a sad reality.

The myth of the unloved daughter isn't that there's no such thing as an unloved daughter (or a mother who doesn't love her daughter). Or that she doesn't struggle in ways that daughters who are loved do not.

The myth is that her life will forever be a sad reality.

In her book *Diana, Herself: An Allegory of Awakening* by Martha Beck, the main character, Diana, was abandoned at birth by her mother, who put her in a garbage dumpster. She was eventually adopted by an abusive couple from whom she ran away. In a fantastical story, Diana meets Herself, a very smart wild boar.

Stay with me here.

"The mirror image of suffering is the truth. Try it. Change the story. Change the course of your entire history. Right now," Herself says.

"You want me to lie about my past?" Diana asks, wiping tears from her face with the back of her hand.

"No, tell the story a truer way," says Herself. "Any story can be told infinite ways, dear, but listen to me. Listen well. If a story liberates your soul, believe it. But if a story imprisons you, believe its mirror image. Use language to free and wild yourself, not keep you tame and in bondage."

Diana used to believe: "They left me because I was a stupid piece of garbage."

The mirror opposite? "I left them. Because I am a brilliant, beautiful treasure."

Diana used to believe: "I wasn't good enough to have parents."

The mirror opposite? "I was too good to have parents."

I did this exercise with a client who shared with me that her mother had told her, more than once: "I never wanted kids and I wish I never had them. My life would have been so much better."

Her mirror opposite?

"All I needed from my parents was to bring me into this amazing world to experience my own life! I'm so emotionally and intuitively deep they couldn't possibly begin to nurture me the way I needed. I had to leave them so I could grow into the woman I want to be."

Inevitably, when I share stories like this, people say things like "Why do mothers say things like that?" and "If women feel that way, why do they have kids in the first place?"

And even "How could a daughter leave her mother?"

These questions are not helpful.

The questions to ask are: How can we challenge, dismantle, and heal internalized misogyny, so that motherhood is no longer a pressure-filled, perfection-demanding role? How can we help girls and women understand that motherhood is their choice and not shame them or pressure them, no matter what choices they make? How can we make motherhood more collaborative and supportive?

I chose not to have children and I can tell you right now that if I'd had the child I was carrying at age twenty-one, I'd have some regrets. I might wish I hadn't had a child.

And? I might even have said it out loud to that child. I have done enough shadow work to know that I am capable of being mean and horrible.

Having a mother who can't or won't love you doesn't have to be a sad reality. You are not doomed. It's not a given, even though we're programmed by society to judge both mothers and daughters when they have a relationship that is considered "less-than." And then, because we don't know what else to say, we reply: *"How sad."*

Nope. Not going to do it.

I am taking this stand with you because I am not willing to let you be a lesser version of yourself.

CHAPTER 19
TAKING YOURSELF ONTO YOUR OWN LAP (A.K.A. RE-MOTHERING)

••

One morning in yoga class, I was crouched down on my tippy-toes with my heels touching. My head was bowed, chin to chest, with my upper body resting on my thighs and my fingertips lightly touching my mat.

The yoga teacher said: "Curl yourself up like a seed and take yourself onto your own lap."

I melted a bit. I experienced a lovely sensation in my chest. And tears pricked my eyes.

Another time, I was sitting in my easy chair, talking with a mentor about something that is hard for me to talk about. I felt myself wanting to shut down.

"Ask your body what it needs," she said.

I leaned forward and took myself onto my own lap.

I melted a bit. I experienced a lovely sensation in my chest. And tears pricked my eyes.

This is how I re-mother myself. I hold space for all of me, even (especially) the parts I might find ugly, shameful, or disgusting. Read on...

* * *

Several years ago I attended a two-day workshop. In the months leading up to it, I was conflicted. Part of me wanted to go, and another part did not. My experience with these types of events is that I go, intending it to be fun and empowering, and then somewhere along the line, I find myself feeling insecure, small, and powerless. It tends to happen so fast that I am blindsided by it.

Then the next time I think, "Oh, I've got this now...it won't happen again." And then it happens again in a slightly different way, but it's all based on the same story: in an effort to impress and/or get the approval of the female authority figure, I will "forget" what I really want and start wanting what I think she thinks I should want. I will show up as needing to be fixed. I will want to impress her and get her validation and approval. And I won't be able to control it.

I was telling my husband about it when these words popped out of my mouth: "As crazy as it sounds, I don't feel 'safe' in those kinds of environments because I feel like I will be forced do something against my will."

And then *bam*, I had a flashback to a time, when I was five or six years old, and my mother and stepfather took me somewhere and we spent the night in a hotel. All I had was my winter nightgown, and it was hot so they gave me one of my stepfather's T-shirts to sleep in instead.

My mother wanted to take a picture of me in his T-shirt. I didn't want her to. I tried to hide in the bathroom and they forced their way in. Then I tried to hide under the bedcovers and they tore them off. As I ran around the room trying to hide, they took pictures of me.

They thought it was funny. I was confused.

After all these years I know what I thought and felt in that moment:

Thought: What I want doesn't matter.

Feeling: violated and powerless.

In that moment—fifty years ago—it was true, but it hasn't been true for a long time, even though I sometimes act as if it is (especially in certain situations where there is a female authority figure).

I rewrote my story this way: I can attend events without those previously unconscious thoughts and emotions running the show. My preferences matter. I get to choose. I have self-agency. I do not betray myself. And? If I have a moment when I find myself feeling that way again, I can take myself onto my own lap. I can ask my inner needy little girl what she needs from me and give it to her.

You can too.

* * *

How do you begin to take yourself onto your own lap? To re-mother yourself?

You can start by mentally and emotionally detaching the woman who gave birth to you from the role of "mother." Your mother will always be your mother, but you can separate yourself, not only from her role, but also from her stories and beliefs.

From the time you were born, and even when you were in the womb, your relationship with your mother was your teacher. It served as a blueprint for your relationship with yourself. Your mother's beliefs were the basis for your own. You learned to treat yourself the way your mother treated herself, and the way she treated you. This is generally a completely unconscious process. You internalize what you experience.

The nature of the mother-daughter relationship is such that it seems to be etched in stone—permanent and unchangeable. Thus, it often feels like your relationship with yourself is the same.

So many of us have an "I'm not good enough" or a "Something is wrong with me" story, and, as you know, I have those stories, too.

Those stories—those beliefs—have played out in my own life in myriad ways, from believing that I wasn't worthy of being loved by a good man (and thus, at age twenty-five I ended up married to a guy from Brazil who needed a green card) to binge eating and spending more money than I had.

As a result, I spent many, many years believing that I couldn't take care of myself. It wasn't until I started practicing acceptance (i.e., not arguing with reality) that I realized I didn't have to believe my mother's stories, nor did I have to blame her for my having adopted them. I simply needed to learn and do differently. And as an adult, this is my choice.

We hear plenty about learning to "mother" ourselves and practicing self-care, and those concepts often seem foreign or confusing. I used to think it meant blaming myself and being super "strict" with myself, such that it would be unpleasant, hard, and involve suffering. This is pretty much the way I was raised, so of course I didn't have anything with which to compare it.

Through years of trial and error, here's what I have learned about re-mothering: It's the ultimate in self-care. It's not about bubble baths and pedicures (although it can include them); it's the deliberate practice of acknowledging, honoring, and meeting your needs and preferences (as you define them), or making sure they get met in a healthy, interdependent way, not in a dysfunctional, codependent, enmeshed way. Meaning, it's your responsibility.

And it requires no force, willpower, manipulation, or bargaining with yourself, or with your mother. Rather than blaming her, or yourself, for all the things that you think are "wrong" with you, you can start to change your internal definitions of what it means to be mothered. Then you can stop looking to an imperfect human female (your mother) for perfect parenting.

Re-mothering can include whatever you need and want it to: acceptance, nurture/care, teaching by example, belonging, confidence, resilience, independence, trust, etc.

Here are some of the ways I re-mother myself (and note that this doesn't happen in a vacuum or in isolation—a key part of re-mothering is being open and receptive to others who can offer you the kind of mothering you desire, knowing when and how to reach out for help, and especially to whom to reach out):

- Not needing to change in order to belong or to be loved, and being able to truly receive love, not only by and from others, but by and from myself;

- Healthy, nourishing food and physical comfort;

- Being discerning and conscious when it comes to the role models and mentors I choose, as well as being a role model for myself—asking myself questions like "How can I like and respect myself in this situation?" and "What would my future self be proud of me for?"; and

- Encouraging emotional confidence, resilience, and independence in myself, not neediness and dependence, and being wary in regard to those who do not encourage me to trust myself.

Once you've separated the idea of "motherhood" from your human mother, you become more open to receiving mothering from a variety of sources, including yourself. Sometimes it requires a bit of "shadow" work to see the areas where you might need a bit of mothering.

Pay attention to the times when you feel pathetic, unlovable, disgusting, empty, needy, stupid, ignorant, helpless, and incapable. These feelings stem from beliefs you have about yourself...the identity you've created. Be honest and open to seeing connections between these feelings and your current circumstances and you will start to see what kind of maternal love can nurture your unmet needs.

Good mothering is available to you if you are willing to let go of expectations that will never be met, and be open to seeing what is offered to you in the moment. Your mother may be limited for whatever reason, but Mother Energy is not.

Re-mothering is shifting away from seeing your mother as limited and blaming her—yet also trying to rely on her— to finding that unconditionally loving Mother Energy within you. Each and every time you do this, you develop and strengthen your emotionally mature, Matriarch Mare, adult self.

This happens as you begin to see the reality of your own lovableness, goodness and value, no matter what's happening out there—no matter what your mother is or isn't doing. You are no longer relying on her for validation or approval.

You are better able to receive love from others because you are no longer invested in seeing yourself as "less-than" in order to be loyal to your mother, and because you are not waiting for her to show up the way you needed or wanted her to.

You are able to see your whole self with compassionate objectivity, which means you acknowledge the faults, flaws, mistakes, while also acknowledging your goodness and value. External approval may come, but you no longer need it to feel okay. Some questions to ask yourself:

- Where do I need to love myself more?
- What am I here to learn?

- What is it that I believe about myself that this situation is showing me?

- What can I do about it?

If there's one thing I want you to do most of all, it's to approach yourself and this process with an attitude of curiosity, fascination, kindness, and compassion. All it requires is a willingness to practice and to understand that just like a little baby learning to walk, you will fall down, and you will want to get right back up and try again. After all, it's exciting, and you desire to see where you might go.

At the same time, you may find yourself grieving and this is perfectly normal and natural. It doesn't mean you're doing it wrong, or taking a step backwards. It's part of the process.

You can become the mother you always wanted for yourself. And you can create a relationship with your mother from a place of acceptance, even if she is no longer here or if you choose not to communicate with her at this time.

Something to consider: Part of re-mothering is learning to retell your story in a way that supports your growth. Below are some journal prompts that will help you redefine who you are now, what you believe, and what you want to believe.

Something to journal on:

- What beliefs, values, and lessons did your mother teach directly (by telling you) and indirectly (via modeling)? Include things you're glad you learned and those you wish you hadn't! Include beliefs about your body, food, sexuality, men, other women, people who are different than you, marriage, money, friendship, etc.

- What do *you* believe and value?

- Are they the same as what your mother taught?

- What do you *want* to believe and value?

- What agreements (usually silent) have you made with your mother without realizing it? Agreements like: "I won't become too successful because I am afraid she'll feel threatened."

- Where did your mother fall short?

- What didn't you receive that you needed and/or wanted?

- How can you start to acknowledge, honor, and meet your own needs and preferences (or get them met)?

- In what areas of your life are you not kind and gentle with yourself?

- How can you demonstrate to yourself (and others, including your own children, if you have them) that you matter?

- What are the consistent, negative thoughts running through your mind?

- Are they your own thoughts or are they your mother's?

CHAPTER 20
RE-MOTHERING IN THE FACE OF BIG EMOTIONS (LIKE SHAME)

One of my earliest experiences with shame was the time—when I was in first grade—that my teacher punished me for calling one of my classmates a crybaby. I had to stay after school and write my numbers, one through one hundred, on the blackboard.

I can remember the hot, prickling feeling on my face, the pit in my stomach, and my shallow breathing.

There was also a sense of "that's not fair!" because I am sure that someone, somewhere along the way, had called me a crybaby. Maybe even my mother. I am pretty sure she didn't use those words, but my little-girl self was full of unresolved, unspoken grief over the divorce of my parents, and my mother was unable to hold space for it.

My emotions were *big*! They were intense and unruly and unpredictable (and they still are sometimes). More than once my parents called me "Sarah Bernhardt," a "diva" actress in the late 1800s who was said to be exaggerated in her willingness to expose her emotions and impose them on her audiences.

I suspect that your mother, my mother, and many other mothers were afraid of our big emotions because they saw "being emotional" as being weak. And if we were weak, we might not survive. Combine that with social conditioning that says women shouldn't show their strength (emotional, physical, intellectual or otherwise) and you've got some serious confusion on your hands.

In the not-so-distant past—in response to a comment someone made to me—I cooked up a complete and total shame meltdown for myself, along with a side of impotent rage. I curled up in bed and sobbed like an irrational, raging, inconsolable child...a big ol' ball of prickly pathetic-ness, shame, grief, and anger all rolled into one. I don't think I have felt that kind of intensity in more than forty years.

My husband (bless his heart) asked if I wanted him to snuggle me. Through my tears I replied, *"Yes, but I'm going to act like I don't."*

This is the epitome of re-mothering—summoning up a modicum of compassion for both myself *and* for him, in that moment, because I know that he needed to be able to comfort me and I needed him.

The big difference between my first-grade self and my now fifty-four-year-old-self is that—even in the depths of seriously uncomfortable emotions—I was...not so much "in control" but aware. With some time and space and some additional re-mothering I gave myself permission to step out of shame and victimhood.

No one is immune to shame.

We all, from time to time, step into victim consciousness.

Normal. Expected. Appropriate. Healthy.

It's not the end of the world.

It proves nothing about us

And we always have the capacity to take exquisite care of our precious selves.

One of the most asked questions I get, when I write about stuff like this is, "Yeah, but *how* do I do that?"

Enter the Train Analogy, which I first read about on a parenting blog, of all places. Katie M. McLaughlin, who has a blog called *Pick Any Two*, says that big, difficult emotions are tunnels, and that we are trains traveling through them. "We have to move all the way through the darkness to get to the—you knew this was coming!—calm, peaceful light at the end of the tunnel. It sounds simple, but it's way easier said than done."

The problem is that our friends, spouses, partners, families, parents, and really, our whole culture are adept at intercepting us on our journeys through the emotional tunnel. We don't like watching other people (especially children) struggle with intense emotion so we try and talk them out of it, or somehow save them from it, because we're trying to make ourselves feel better.

And when we do that, we also intercept their resilience.

Katie goes on to write: "What we adults often do when facing our own emotional struggles is attempt to get out of the tunnel early—banging on the sides, ignoring the cavernous echo, and wondering with confusion why we can't see daylight yet.

Sometimes we squat in the darkness, close our eyes, and just pretend we're not in a tunnel at all. Everything is just fine, thank you very much. Sometimes we do a whole host of other things—eat ice cream, drink wine, shop online, run marathons, binge-watch Netflix, play games on our phones or scroll mindlessly through Facebook—to distract ourselves from the fact that we're in a tunnel in the first place. But none of those things gets us out of the tunnel, does it?"

It's when we finally let ourselves cry and sob and stamp our feet and pound our fists into our pillows without judgment that we not only finally feel so much better, but are able to mobilize our best and show ourselves how resilient we actually are. We can melt down and thrive on the other side of it.

Something to remember: Emotions (as we learned in Chapter 9) are nothing more and nothing less than a vibration in your body. When you intercept them, you intercept your own resilience.

Something to journal on: When it comes to you and your precious self, how can you provide yourself comfort through the big emotions? How can you show compassion and empathy for your struggle? What would feel good and right?

Something to practice: Notice when others are experiencing and/or expressing big emotions. Practice being present for them as they travel through their tunnels. Now try doing it for yourself.

CHAPTER 21
A RADICAL WAY TO BANISH
SHAME FROM YOUR LIFE

••

In April 2015, Elizabeth Gilbert wrote an epic Facebook post about tribal shame and the work of Dr. Mario Martinez, who wrote a book called *The Mind-Body Code*.

He studies the ways our thoughts and emotions affect our physical health and he is particularly interested in the harmful ways that shame affects the mind and body.

Liz Gilbert's post is *so* worth the read, but the short version is this: "...if you dare to leave your tribe of origin—or if you dare to question the rules of your tribe—it is extremely likely that you will be punished. Sometimes that punishment can be violent and extreme.... But oftentimes the punishment is more subtle.... The weapon they are most likely to use against you is shame. Shame is how they keep you in line. Shame is how they let you know that you have abandoned the collective."

It wasn't until about six months later that I made the connection and saw that this is exactly what had happened between my mother and me. It also dawned on me that I had spent most of my life believing (unconsciously) that my mother had the power to destroy me.

So I spent a lot of time bending and contorting myself to get her love and approval, because I feared her disapproval (which in my mind equaled destruction). I also hid from her, especially if I suspected that she wouldn't like or approve of something I had done. Even though I didn't think, intellectually, that she would actually and literally kill me, in my body it *felt* like a possibility.

Here's where it gets interesting. Because of the training I've received and the work I have done on this issue (which includes studying the concept of victim consciousness), I knew whether it was possible or not didn't really matter.

In the past, I would have gone into victim mode. I would have used the revelation as an excuse and a reason to believe my mother is/was evil and that I needed to protect myself.

Instead, I chose to notice how this thought and the resultant emotion(s) had been showing up all over my life, for years. I asked myself if it was serving me (*hell no!*). Slowly, over the course of a couple of months, the fear started to melt away, and the belief that she has the power to destroy me started to wither and die. What once was etched in stone is now ghostly...sort of like something written on an Etch-A-Sketch and then shaken off.

Getting back to Liz Gilbert's post...

In it she outlined an exercise that Dr. Martinez created to help people liberate themselves from fear and shame and it occurred to me that you might find this exercise helpful. I have modified it to suit us.

Step 1: Sit quietly and allow your mind and your breathing to settle. Acknowledge in your mind that you need(ed) to abandon your mother in order to live your life the way you want. Acknowledge that she felt/will feel betrayed.

Step 2: Say, aloud: "Mom, I am going to abandon you now. I am going to betray you now."

Liz says this is powerful because you are saying the opposite of what you have probably spent your life trying to prove: that you haven't betrayed or abandoned your mother. You may have even made yourself sick trying to prove that you are loyal, that you have done nothing wrong, that you haven't changed.

But it doesn't work because she doesn't believe you. Because she knows (and you know, too) that when you chose a different way for yourself, you betrayed and abandoned her. You changed because you needed to. You left her behind because that was the only way to become the person you were meant to be.

And? It's *all* good. Why? Because it doesn't mean that you don't love her.

As Liz said, *"this exercise has nothing to do with love."* You can always love your mother. This exercise is about breaking the spell of shame and the only way to do that is to take ownership of your life, and to admit to the consequences of leaving your mother's values behind.

Step 3: Become your mother (in your mind). Say to yourself (in her voice) these words: *"I completely understand. I forgive you. All I want is for you to be happy."*

149

It's important that you hold both sides of this imagined conversation.

Step 4: Rebuild what Dr. Martinez calls your own "field of honor." Shaming works because it attacks your sense of honor. Liz Gilbert puts it this way: "Every tribe is governed by its own code of honor, and once you have broken that honor code, the tribe will accuse you (overtly or subtly) of having no honor at all. This accusation is what makes you sick. This is what makes you suffer."

So you must rebuild your own field of honor, in order to make yourself healthy again.

You do this by making a list of all the times you have been honorable, starting as young as you can remember. What was the first honorable act of your life? Go from there and write down all the ways in which you have been honorable.

"You are truly an honorable person. Honor is within you. You must rebuild that field of honor, because it is your only defense against shaming, which will always seek to destroy your sense of honor in order to make you weak and to bring you back 'home.'"

S ep 5: Feel righteous anger (and note here that I am not suggesting that you act on it...just *feel* it).

You will know that you are standing in your field of honor when your first reaction to attempts to shaming you are righteous anger. You will know that you are on the road to emotional health and recovery when [your mother] tries to shame you, and rather than absorb that shame, you instead react with righteous anger.

Dr. Martinez suggests that there is a role in your life for healthy anger, for appropriate anger, for righteous anger. Righteous anger is a fast, hot fire that burns up the poison of shaming, and protects your field of honor. This is the anger that rises up like a dragon and says, "Don't you *dare* try to shame me!" This anger is correct and just and fair. You are entitled to it. You must claim it.

You are a person of honor who does not deserve to be shamed. Righteous anger protects you from judging yourself when your mother tries to shame you so learn how to *feel* it when and if you experience shaming.

Repeat after me: *"I do not deserve to be shamed!"*

Practice as often as you need.

CHAPTER 22
WHEN YOU DECIDE TO CHANGE

The process of choosing to wake up and change wasn't easy on me, or on my mother. As of this writing, our relationship consists mostly of birthday cards or calls (or not) and an email here or there.

After several years of no contact, we began a shaky back-and-forth via email. It was an excellent opportunity for me to practice the concepts I've outlined in this book. We got together in person during the summer of 2014. The visit had its good moments, as well as some tense ones, as I chose to maintain my boundaries. There were some conversations I wasn't willing to have, and I let her know that those subjects were none of my business. (And yes, I mean "my" business. In this case she wanted to have a conversation about another family member whom she believed had betrayed her. It wasn't my business!)

Additionally, I explained to her that I was letting her off the hook for having to approve of me, I was no longer making her responsible for my feelings, and I was also not taking responsibility for hers. I said, "If you want to feel disappointed or ashamed of me, that's on you."

When we said our goodbyes, she asked, "Does this mean we can call each other and see each other again?" I replied, "Of course."

That didn't happen, although we continued to communicate via email. In the spring of 2015 I asked if she'd like to get together again. Her response indicated that she didn't see the point in it, and further, that she felt uncomfortable being around me.

It stung. I cried. Hard, heaving, can't-catch-my-breath sobs. The little girl in me felt rejected by her mommy. I immediately wanted to call/email/post on social media to anyone who would listen and say...

"See?! Look what's she's done to me now!"

I was creating a reason to have my "story" playing (un) happily in the background again, rather than creating a new one. The adult me, however, felt relieved. And then guilty, because I was relieved in part—and also because, deep down inside, I wanted her to reject me so I wouldn't have to be the bad guy. I also observed it provided the opportunity for a massive pity-party!

So perhaps part of me wanted something like this to happen, so I could continue to be "right" about her. Yet another part of me was feeling guilty for having "abandoned" my mother when I had become more emotionally grounded and mature. Maybe I created this dynamic so she would reject or punish me? Or maybe I was just putting the ball in her court, allowing her to be the one to choose the engagement between the two of us? It was easy to think myself into a circle around all of this.

Within the space of about an hour (rather than days, weeks, months...years), I went from pity-me-mode (helpless little girl who can't take care of herself), into go-to-hell-mode (channeling my inner rebellious teenager), and into pretend-evolved-adult-mode ("I am so above this"), and right back to pity again.

That's when I caught myself in the middle of my own damned pattern and actually laughed out loud. Thanks to my mother, I got to see just how good my mind has gotten at going for pity. I could practically feel the neurons firing down the well-worn pathways in my brain. My brain likes pity.

And so I asked myself, "Who do I want to be in this moment? What can I say that will allow me to like myself?" My answer: I want to be a non-reactive, non-defensive, non-pity-seeking grown-ass woman who chooses to love her mother without indulging in the drama. I want to be free.

I want to be the Matriarch Mare.

So I hit reply and wrote, "Okay, let me know if you change your mind."

I am free.

When you change the parameters of the way you behave in your relationship with your mother, your mother might not like it, she may fight it to some degree, or be puzzled by it. There will be some wobbly tension while new boundaries and patterns are put into place. This is a very, very common experience.

Something to consider: While you can't control your mother, or how she might react to you choosing to change, you can choose to be okay. That's not a guarantee that you will never be sad or angry again, but rather that you will have your own back. You will know how to handle whatever emotions arise as you navigate your relationship with your mother and yourself. Knowing that you get to choose how you want to feel is the most empowering aspect of this process because it puts you in the driver's seat of your life.

CHAPTER 23
CHOOSING UNCONDITIONAL LOVE

So now that you understand the nature of your thoughts and emotions—and how they are connected—let me ask you this: How do you want to feel about your mother? Of all the feelings that are available to you, which might you choose?

I'm guessing that love isn't on your list. It certainly wasn't on mine.

At first, I thought it was unlikely that I could ever love my mother, or stop feeling danger surrounding her. As I've said, I spent years feeling chronic anger, bitterness, and resentment towards my mother. Although I knew it wasn't good for me, I believed that those emotions protected me. I understood that it was possible to get past the negative feelings, but I was afraid that if I let those feelings go, she would "win"—and I would end up giving in to whatever she wanted and would always have to agree with her, which meant that I'd never escape from her abusive or dysfunctional behavior. I wanted to love her, but I didn't know how to do that and preserve myself at the same time.

Back then, it was an either/or proposition: either I stay angry and protect myself, or I "love" her and let her swallow me whole—at least, that's what it felt like was happening at the time. That's because I didn't understand that love is an emotion that I can choose to feel—not a concept, action, or behavior that is forced on me or even expected of me.

All emotions—from fear and anger to joy and love—are nothing more and nothing less than vibrations that we feel in our bodies. Shame usually comes with a hot, prickly feeling around my face and neck. Grief is an exquisite ache in my throat and heart. Anger feels like the wind has been knocked out of me (and it's heavy too), and I feel slightly choked. Anxiety is weak knees, shallow breathing, and a shakiness in my belly.

And love? It's a heart-melting, warm sensation in my chest and belly. The more I understand about love, the more I know that it's not an emotion that comes with conditions. I can create it and feel it simply because I want to.

And because I like the way love feels, I make a conscious choice to feel it when I think about my mother (and I am not talking about it in a "love and light" woo woo spiritual by-passing way), rather than choosing anger, bitterness, and resentment (which don't feel so great). I also choose to have amazing boundaries.

When you choose to feel love, you get to feel love—without conditions. Which isn't to say that you take responsibility for how your mother feels, or for her reputation. It doesn't mean you have to spend time with her or talk to her if you don't want to. You don't have to be friendly or pretend to like her. You don't have to do what she says.

Now that you've learned how to notice what you're feeling, and how to connect those feelings to the thoughts you are thinking, rather than attaching them to what your mother says or does, you get to choose.

What has most helped me to choose love is understanding that my mother doesn't have to change in order for me to feel it. There are no conditions. It's my responsibility, not hers. I don't have to rely on her to do anything in order for me to feel it. As a result of choosing to feel love for my mother, I get to feel it, and I like how it feels.

I've also established boundaries that come from a place of love and respect for both of us. And most importantly, when I let her off the hook for being responsible for my feelings (but not for her actions), I also let myself off the hook for being responsible for hers. We are two autonomous women. A mother and a daughter. Powerful in our own separate rights.

Something to consider: Most people equate love with tolerating bad behavior. How about this instead: Love is always an available choice. You don't always have to choose it, but you always have the choice. Love doesn't know the difference between conditional and unconditional. Loving does not mean tolerating bad behavior or not having boundaries—in fact, I'd say good boundaries are part of what allows love to thrive. Even if you choose never to see or speak to your mother again, you can choose to feel love when you think about her.

Something to practice:

- Close your eyes and take a deep breath. Unlock those shoulders. Soften your eyes. Take another deep breath.

- Think about someone or something that you love. Think of how much happiness this person or thing brings to your life and how much you love them.

- Continue focusing on this person or thing until you start to feel a physical sensation. Describe it. Where in your body do you feel it? Does it have a texture? A temperature? A color?

- Now think about someone for whom it's hard to feel love. Summon up any anger, resentment, and bitterness you have towards this person until you start to feel it physically. Get to know it, just like you got to know what unconditional love feels like. Which feels better?

- Understand that choosing to feel unconditional love is a favor you do for yourself. It's available to you right now if you want it.

- Understand that loving unconditionally does not mean tolerating bad behavior from others, or even having to see or speak to someone. It just means that when you think of this person, you choose to still feel amazing.

CHAPTER 24
WHAT'S ON THE OTHER SIDE OF THE STRUGGLE?

I don't remember a time that I didn't struggle, on some level, in my relationship with my mother. Throughout this book I have shared some examples. One of my earliest memories is of me sitting in my high chair, crying with rage and shock, because she'd dumped a bowl of cereal and milk over my head—apparently because I was being stubborn and wouldn't finish it.

A more recent memory: the time I smiled at her through an open window, and she sneered and gave me the finger (yes, that one).

Hopelessness. Helplessness. Anxiety. Self-loathing. Impotent rage. Blame and shame. Oh, the blame and the shame. Blaming myself, blaming my mother. Being ashamed for blaming. 'Round and 'round it went.

As you now know, intense emotions can lead you to do some pretty dramatic things. For me, it was binge eating, looking for love in all the wrong places, spending money I didn't have until I was significantly in debt and had to declare bankruptcy, trying to control others to the point where I nearly damaged important relationships, and, at times, lashing out at people I love.

And on a more subtle but certainly profound level, I held myself back from fully exploring, using, and sharing my gifts and talents. I kept wondering who and what I could have been (if only...) or believing that so much of my time had been wasted "asleep at the wheel" of my life. I was lamenting, but without believing it could be otherwise. And then, in a misguided effort to not struggle in my relationship with my mother, I cut her out of my life and actually found myself giving it more of my time, attention, and energy.

And I can tell you right now, it didn't feel good...not deep down inside where it matters. Even though I was telling myself otherwise, I was not free. I was not at peace.

(I'll say it again, because it's important: For some daughters, the very best, most freeing, peaceful thing to do might actually be to sever ties with their mothers. If that's the case, I encourage you to do it from as clean a place as possible, meaning that you're doing it not because you believe you have no other choice, but rather because, for now, you know you can't show up in the relationship in a way that you like and respect.)

I knew I needed and wanted something more for myself. It was time to heal on a deeper level. (Those of you who read my first book know that my first conscious healing journey concerned finding peace with food and my body.) Many of the same tools that served me then have served me as I do this deeper healing.

And so I did the work on this issue, too (and I will continue to do it, because it is ongoing, for all of us). I asked myself the hard questions, and more importantly, I answered them. And the answers have been profoundly satisfying. For the first time in my life, I know what it's like to...

- live my life without the constant negative thoughts about my mother;

- live without thinking that she should approve of my life;

- show up in the world as myself and not "in reaction" to her; and

- be unafraid of her.

And although my mother and I have been estranged at times, I don't have to wait for her to die to feel differently. More than one woman has told me that it wasn't until her mother died that she finally felt free. Knowing what I know now, I see that feeling free is not dependent on my mother dying. It isn't dependent on anyone or anything other than myself. True freedom comes from your mind. No one can set you free...only you have the power to do that.

So, somewhere along the line, I decided that I was going to set myself free—whether or not my mother is alive, whether or not my mother approves. So what does it look like to feel free?

Imagine not holding yourself back from creating what you want (because you're afraid of what your mother will say).

Imagine being able to say "no" without apology or explanation.

Imagine being able to set boundaries that serve you and strengthen the relationships that mean the most to you.

Imagine taking good care of your physical, mental, spiritual, and emotional self.

Imagine being able to meet your own needs and being able to ask for help in doing so.

Imagine not sabotaging your efforts.

Imagine not having to force yourself.

Imagine not hurting yourself.

Imagine setting goals from a place of excitement, without having them be attached to what others think.

Imagine being able to ask yourself how you want to show up in the world, knowing that it's always your choice, and then doing it.

Imagine not being afraid to share yourself and your work (sure, you might be nervous—but you can handle it).

Imagine not being afraid to "go there" and understanding that "going there" isn't as painful and scary as *not* "going there" is.

Imagine being able to make mistakes and fail without spiraling into shame and hopelessness.

Imagine being able to have doubts and confusion, knowing it's temporary, even though it sucks in the moment.

Imagine having your own sweet back.

Imagine loving your amazing self.

And now? Imagine the positive impact of this on future generations. Our mothers may not have been able to model for us what we needed them to, but there's no reason we can't stretch now.

CHAPTER 25
DEAR MOTHERS OF WOMEN WHO ARE READING THIS BOOK

I'm betting that when your daughter talks about the strained relationship she has with you, you make it mean that she thinks you are a bad mother—maybe even a bad person—and that she's the one who has suffered as a result. You might even make it mean that she thinks she's the "good one" in the relationship.

Here's the thing: she's just different.

Because she needed and wanted your love and approval her whole life, she sometimes contorted, changed, and hid herself. She did this not because she thought what she was doing was bad or wrong (because it wasn't)—she did it because she was afraid that if you knew the real her, you would withdraw your love.

And now that she's being her true self, it seems like she's changed! She's not as pliable and malleable. She's not as easily manipulated, and it's caused some friction—or maybe even estrangement.

Here's what you need to know about your daughter: She needs and wants to feel good about herself and her life, but she didn't have the self-discipline to do that when she was enmeshed with you.

Because you were so big and so important to her, she gave you an inordinate amount of her attention. And in so doing, without meaning to, you trained her to separate herself from herself. She loved you so much and stayed enmeshed with you a long time because she thought she might be able to find herself anyway. But as it turned out, she couldn't.

She couldn't not be herself (for you) and be herself (for herself) at the same time.

So she figured, at a minimum, that she needed space because of her lack of self-discipline. She needed space so she could retrain herself back into alignment with who she is...and who she wants to be.

She loves her life. She feels good about herself. She likes to wake up every day and feel alive and on purpose. She wants to talk about happy things, and she wants to see the best in others. She wants to feel good about what she gives her attention to. And for a while, when she was with you, she was able to do that. But the longer the two of you were together and the more enmeshed the two of you became, the less able she was to do that. It became a struggle, and the struggle sucked the life out of her.

So here's the plan. She is going to choose to feel fabulous. And she is going to do everything in her power to envision you feeling fabulous, too. She could write pages and pages about all the things she loves about you, but she is *not* responsible for how you feel...and you've tried to make her responsible for that every damned day. That's not her job, it's yours.

Her promise to you is that she will be as happy as she can and will never hold you responsible for the way she feels.

Also, please know that I see *you*.

I see your hurt and fear.

I understand that you might think I am trying to drive an even deeper wedge between you and your daughter.

I understand that you might believe your daughter is looking to me to absolve her of responsibility.

I acknowledge that you think I am only hearing one side of the story and that we're ganging up on you.

I also understand that your daughter has, perhaps, been abusive towards you. Your daughter might be difficult. I was a difficult daughter and, perhaps, my mother still thinks I am.

The work I do is not about creating divisiveness between you and your daughter, or turning your daughter against you. It's about helping your daughter discover and take responsibility for her own beliefs, thoughts, and feelings—separate from yours.

My devotion is helping your daughter become the creative, confident, unflappable woman she wants to be.

So when I talk about separation, it's not about disrespect or never seeing each other, it's about both of you becoming emotionally autonomous women who have healthy, respectful boundaries.

One thing I know for sure is that, whereas I used to hate myself, I now love and respect myself, and that love and respect extends outward from me to my mother.

When I was able to take responsibility for my thoughts and emotions, I was able to also take responsibility for my actions and to stop blaming her. That is ultimately what I teach—in my writings, in my support calls, in my workshops, and in the one-on-one coaching I do.

This is where our freedom, peace, and happiness lies. It can be hard work, and a woman has to be ready, willing, and able to do it. It was both the hardest and the very best thing I've ever done for myself.

So fear not, dear mothers of the women who are reading my book.

Your daughter is a woman, just like you.

This book is as much for you as it is for her.

CHAPTER 26
Q&A WITH KAREN

Dear Karen,

I am filled with angst after a recent conversation with my mother. I have a feeling my story is one you've heard before.

My mother divorced my father when I was six. It is widely acknowledged that he slept around and had anger issues—and poor coping skills—but he was a hard worker. Even though she eventually married a good man and had a long marriage, throughout my life my mother incessantly berated my father to me and then would say, "But remember, he's still your father."

After decades of hearing how he cheated on and abused her, I learned to not like my father and failed to see anything positive in him. I did come to terms with him as flawed person who did the best he could.

My mother is elderly now and has some dementia. She occasionally gets in a dig about my father. She recently asked for a copy of his obituary. Upon reading it, she called me to continue criticizing him. I felt so hurt. I knew it was fruitless to ask her to stop saying things about him because I've asked dozens of times over the years, telling her it feels like a stab in the heart every time she badmouths him.

I try to distance myself from the feelings, but they're still there, even as I write this. I don't know if it's because I take her

*criticism of him to heart...no daughter wants to see his father
act this way.*

* * *

Yes, I do know this one. A lot of women do. A day that
is seared in my memory is the time my mother said to
me, "Karen, your father is a total loser!" after I asked her
whether, if she had to go back and choose, she would
choose my father or my stepfather (both of whom she
had divorced).

I cried harder and longer than ever before in my life (I am
not exaggerating).

What I know now, that I didn't know then, is that my
despair, grief, and anger were caused not by what she said,
but rather by what I made her words mean: that I was the
result of a casual mistake. I interpreted her words as being
dismissive and full of contempt. Which isn't to say that I
am blaming myself, or that I believe it's okay for a mother
to say that to her daughter.

Something else I know now, that I didn't then, is that
my mother and I were emotionally enmeshed—our
relationship was boundary-less. If I'd had better
boundaries, I wouldn't have asked her such a question,
and if she'd had better boundaries, she would have
handled it differently. It's not something I beat myself up
for (any more) and nor do I blame her (any more).

Now, I choose not ask my mother those kinds of questions.
And if she were to criticize or berate my father to me, I'd

let her know that the subject isn't up for discussion. My boundaries in that regard are impeccable.

So while it might be fruitless to expect your mother to stop saying negative things about your father, it's not fruitless to ask her not to.

Here are two types of boundary conversations you might have (look back at Chapter 13 for a detailed explanation and exploration of these two "request" techniques, along with other tips and ideas about impeccable boundaries):

(1) *Request–Benefit Conversation:* Mom, I'd appreciate it if you wouldn't say negative things to me about my father. Our relationship would be stronger if we avoided that topic. (Modify to suit your preferences.)

(2) *Request–Consequence Conversation:* Mom, please don't say negative things to me about my father. If you continue, I will hang up the phone (or leave the room, etc.).

As well, you can ask yourself what you are making it mean when your mother says negative things to you about your father. In so doing, you might find some peace.

What do you think?

Much, much love,
Karen

* * *

Dear Karen,

How do I deal with the fact that my mother is gossiping about me and turning everyone in my family against me?

It is hard to know that your mother is saying unkind things about you that aren't true.

So let's pretend that everything she says or does is the result of everything she has ever experienced in her life including the way her parents treated her, her fears, defenses, beliefs, and so on.

Let's also pretend that all of that has nothing to do with you, even if what she says seems directly aimed at you or is about you.

And finally, let's assume that she's suffering, even though it might not appear that way. Saying unkind, untrue things is a form of suffering.

(Think about that for a second...)

Saying unkind, untrue things is a form of suffering.

This does not mean that her suffering is your responsibility. It's just a signal to you. A moment to pause, take a breath, and ask yourself: "What do I believe? What do I *want* to believe? How do I want to feel? How do I want to show up in this moment?"

In this way, you will experience less suffering and more freedom.

As you practice not taking anything that your mother says or does personally, you may find that she stops. You will see that it's only abuse when you believe what she is saying and take on her suffering. You will know that your reputation and worth are not determined by what your mother says, does, or believes.

And if necessary, you can walk away without creating more suffering for yourself, and without having to convince her that you are a good and worthy daughter.

You are worthy because you exist.

As for the rest of your family...

> "...if we want to be free, we have to let everybody be free. I hate and resent this so much. It means we have to let the people in our families and galaxies be free to be asshats, if that is how they choose to live. This however, does not mean we have to have lunch with them. Or go on vacation with them again. But we do have to let them be free." —Anne Lamott

Gotta love Anne for expressing herself authentically.

Much, much love,
Karen

* * *

Dear Karen,

Navigating this "no contact" thing is tricky. I feel better and know it's in my best interest, but my mom has roped both my dad and sister into this mess, which is making "no contact" increasingly difficult and a huge stressor in my life. She refuses to reach out to me, my dad hasn't reached out to me, and she asks my sister every day if she has spoken to me. In addition, my mom is now posting passive-aggressive "motivational quotes" on Facebook, stuff like "I only need someone in my life if they need me in theirs."

What I'm struggling with is how to initiate that contact again. I don't want this to spin out of control, and I've already been no contact for a month. I'm trying to stick to my guns, but am fearful since others are now involved. I don't want things to get out of hand. I don't know if I'm in fact ready to begin my relationship with her again, even though I have all this new knowledge regarding narcissism and her control over my thoughts and feelings. I don't want to jump in before I'm ready to create borders and have my own back, but I also don't like this feeling I have of the three of them against me.

Any advice or help is greatly appreciated! Thank you!

Let me preface my response by saying what I always say: my job is to help you navigate your life on your own terms (versus telling you what to do)...and for those of us who have "mommy issues" this can be both uncomfortable and a breath of fresh and welcome air.

So let's pretend that we're sitting together over a cuppa whatever, okay?

First let me share my own story...maybe it can help you decide if what I did is right for you.

When I (ostensibly) cut ties with my mother at the end of 2010 (because of something she said to me in an email that I deemed "the final straw"), I thought it was forever. That's what I intended at the time because I was so through with her...dysfunction.

Although I didn't have the language for it at the time, what I see now is that I was emotionally enmeshed with her (meaning, I unconsciously believed that she caused my feelings, whether I was in her presence or not); I was still "tied" to her even though we didn't see or talk to one another. I thought about her a lot and I talked about her to anyone who would listen.

A few years later, when I was learning many of the skills and tools I now teach, I was excited to put them into practice, believing they would "fix" the situation and that "fixing" the situation would make it "all better." I have to (kindly) laugh at myself now when I think about it.

What I didn't realize is that the only thing that would truly make me feel better was focusing on me: my thoughts, my emotions, my actions. I didn't want to do that at first because I was living both "in reaction" and "in resistance" to my mother. It's almost like I wasn't aware that I even had my own thoughts and emotions!

I didn't trust myself because I didn't know who I was, apart from her.

Taking a break from our relationship helped me get to know myself. And in so doing, I became more "me." I like, respect, and trust myself so much more, whether I am in her presence or not. I am grounded in my values and preferences.

So, in regard to your question—how to initiate contact again—here are some questions to consider:

- Why do you want to reinitiate contact?
- What are your hopes for doing so?
- Do you like and respect your reasons?
- What values are important to you?
- What are your preferences?
- How can you show yourself kindness?
- What boundaries do you need to have in place?
- Do you trust yourself to honor your boundaries if they are crossed?

Ultimately this is about trusting yourself and focusing on what you want and need—right now. Women are generally not rewarded for doing that in our culture (in fact, they are often subtly punished), so there's a lot of fear and guilt associated with it.

Showing yourself kindness doesn't mean that you're being unkind to them. Kindness never fails.

And finally, no matter what choice you make now, you can always change it. Rest in that.

Much, much love,
Karen

P.S. You might want to unfollow your mother on Facebook. ;-)

* * *

Dear Karen,

What do you do with a dysfunctional mother-daughter relationship once the mother passes away? I thought I would be "okay" with my mother's passing, but truth be told, I am not doing as well as I would like. Self talk turns negative far too frequently, then anger usually sneaks its ugly nose into my thoughts. I want to believe in and hold onto the positive memories, but what was supposed to be a healing opportunity has ended up with a deeper realization of bitterness and hurt! Suggestions?

As complicated as mother-daughter relationships can be when they're alive, when our mothers die, it can become even more complex.

My number one piece of advice is to not judge yourself or your emotions (whether they're "positive" or "negative"). You're human and you're built to experience the full range of human emotion.

Also consider that there is no such thing as the "wrong" emotion.

We create additional suffering for ourselves when we believe that we "should" feel a certain way when someone dies...*especially* our mothers! And if what we're feeling isn't what we think we should be feeling, then there must be something wrong with us.

Emotions are not proof of anything—they're just a vibration in your body that is the result of something you are thinking.

Sometimes that vibration is uncomfortable. Anger, bitterness, and hurt can be unpleasant. Perhaps there's some regret and guilt thrown in for good measure. Add grief on top of it all...and wow, you've got a pretty potent mixture.

None of these emotions mean that you're bad or that you're not healing or that something has gone wrong. All they mean is that you're human.

All of that being said, feeling those unpleasant (and sometimes downright painful) emotions on the regular isn't appealing.

So here are five steps to feel better:

Step 1: Be aware. Pay attention to the way those uncomfortable emotions actually feel in your body and notice them with compassion. Do not judge yourself or the emotions (for example, anger isn't ugly). Try not to distract yourself or pretend that they're not there.

Step 2: Allow. Allow the emotion to just be there. Try not to resist, react, or distract. Release the resistance, reaction, or distraction. Be willing to be uncomfortable.

Step 3: Acknowledge. Name the emotion—say it out loud or write it down. The more specific you can get, the better. Instead of just saying, "I feel down," find the specific one-word description: I'm pissed/bitter/hurt/sad/relieved/ grieving/regretful. Consciously recognizing negative emotions reduces their impact.

Step 4: Describe. Describe the experience of the emotion as if you were explaining it to a Martian who has no clue what an emotion is (where is it in your body? what color is it? does it have a texture? a temperature? what does it feel like, physically?).

Step 5: Give yourself permission. When you give yourself permission to feel those negative emotions, you might find that some positive feelings follow.

The vast majority of the time, this process will make any emotion dissipate within a matter of minutes. It's just a vibration that flows through you and then it's gone.

There are times when it doesn't go away as quickly (and grief is one of those emotions). There might be a feeling of heaviness, depression, or anxiety that stays with you. Again, this doesn't mean you're not doing it right...you might have to go through these five steps many times.

Something to consider: Choosing to be compassionate with yourself and those emotions will ebb and flow like waves. They will eventually dissipate much more quickly than if you resist, react, or distract.

Something to journal on: What are you making it mean (about you, about your mother, about your relationship) that you are feeling anger, bitterness, and hurt after her death? Is there another way you could look at it that might feel better? What is it?

Something to practice: Simply place your hands over your heart. This is a small act of self-compassion that has shown to calm the fight/flight response in the brain and re-engage the creative, problem-solving part.

Grieve well.

Much, much love,
Karen

* * *

Dear Karen,

My mother makes the most offensive comments. She makes snide remarks about my weight (whether I've gained or lost), my hair (it's too "wild"), my kids (because I am not raising them the way she raised me), my husband (he's "too quiet")...you name it.

I try not to let it bother me. Sometimes I am successful and sometimes I'm not and I blow up. But if I am honest, even when I don't blow up it always *bothers me. How can I let it go?*

I think this is probably the most universal mother-daughter issue there is.

In fact, when I received this question, I decided to ask some of my friends and clients the question, "What are some of the most offensive things your mother has ever said to you?"

Here are some of their answers:

"It's about time" or "He was supposed to do that." (While acting overly surprised and making a big deal when my husband does something around the house, because he doesn't contribute enough to her liking.)

"You should be ashamed of yourself."

"How come your hips are still big?" (After I lost thirty-five pounds.)

"Shame on you. Who do you think you are? Don't be impertinent. You are such a prima donna." (Along with a combination eye-roll / shake of the head / clicking noise with a sigh when she was annoyed/disappointed.)

"If I reached for seconds on food, she would sometimes make a piggy snorting noise."

"You'll never know how much turmoil you put me through."

"You really look like crap!" (When I was thirty-two, wasn't wearing any makeup, and stopped coloring my hair.)

"Do you think you're a dog? When you get out of the shower, you just shake your head and then your hair is ready to go?"

"You have a bubble butt."

"Now I know why your husband divorced you."

"I'm really glad you didn't have another child."

When we're children (even well into our early twenties) our prefrontal cortex (the "higher" part of our brain that is able to reason and think more objectively) is not fully developed, so we have a tendency to take everything personally...to make everything that happens (and everything that anyone says) mean something about us.

It's normal and natural for a daughter (even an adult daughter) to seek her mother's validation and approval. So when our mothers say something to us and we make it mean that she doesn't approve...well, that's when we find ourselves feeling offended, hurt, annoyed, and perhaps even unworthy. We revert and our now fully developed prefrontal cortexes are overtaken by the more primitive part of our brains.

Generally speaking, if you're offended by something your mother says to you *about* you (or your kids or your partner), it's probably because you (1) believe her (on some level) and/or (2) think what she said is negative or "bad."

If you didn't believe what she said, and if you didn't think what she said is negative, you wouldn't be offended.

I know it's not easy to unravel years and years of ingrained belief, but once you're aware you have a belief that doesn't serve you, and if you allow yourself to be curious enough to notice when and where these beliefs show up (and how they feel in your body) it's like that saying: what has been seen can't be unseen.

Once you're aware, you can't be unaware. And that's where the magic lies!

So how to begin?

1. Pick one thing your mother said to you that you find offensive and write it down.

2. Ask yourself why it's important to you that your mother not say this (you can go deeper and ask yourself why it's important that she approve of you in this specific circumstance).

3. Do you believe what she said is true? If yes, why?

4. Do you believe what she said is negative or bad? If yes, why?

5. What do you want to believe regarding this thing your mother has said?

6. How does it feel to believe that?

7. Reframe it. "My mother said [insert whatever she said here]. I don't agree with her, nor do I think that [insert whatever she said here] is a bad thing. What I want to believe is [insert what you believe here].

8. Can you find evidence for what you want to believe? Write it down.

Speaking from personal experience, once I let my mother off the hook for validation and approval, the easier it became for me to not react.

Much, much love,
Karen

CHAPTER 27
HOW DOES THIS BOOK END?

So here we are, at the end of the book. You are not the same woman you were when you started reading. And I am certainly not the same woman I was when I started writing.

What has changed? What is your new reality? What is your new story? What boundaries have you set? What promises have you made to yourself? What promises have you kept?

Where have you stopped "shoulding" when it comes to yourself and your mother? How have you started taking care of yourself and meeting your own needs? Are you practicing freedom and autonomy? Where do you need to practice more?

You may feel a bit nervous and adrift, wondering if you can really do this on your own. My wish for you is, no matter how you choose to do it, that you make yourself a priority and do this work for you, not for your mother. What I know for sure is that the awareness you cultivate is priceless.

I once heard a woman at a workshop say, "When you can stand on your story, and not let your story stand on you, you'll be able to truly help others. You'll know, deep down inside, your 'why.'"

Here's my "why." I am passionate about helping women transform their mother stories because:

The world needs women who are truly impressed with themselves and who are excited to create (and I don't mean in an artistic way, unless that's the way their creativity manifests itself). When women are impressed with themselves, they do amazing things in the world.

They are amazing (not perfect) friends, partners, wives, mothers, sisters. They are confident, and they strive to make a difference, not from a place of desperation or needing to prove something, but from a place of pure joy and aliveness.

When women are impressed with themselves, they are amazing scientists, teachers, dancers, politicians, writers, engineers, poets, and businesspeople.

When women are impressed with themselves, they are happy in their own skin. They take excellent care of themselves and are thus able to nurture others.

When women are impressed with themselves, whatever they want to do is okay.

They are examples of what is possible.

But because of patterns and stories that get passed down, mother to daughter (especially in a dysfunctional, patriarchal culture), some women are afraid to be impressed with themselves—and they are afraid to create, afraid to shine, afraid to put themselves first.

I had a mutually abusive, dysfunctional, codependent, and enmeshed relationship with my mother. As a result of that, I told myself a whopper of a story about me, a story that based on me for years. That story went something like this: I am pathetic. I am bad. I am unworthy. I can't trust myself. I can't take care of myself. I should be ashamed of myself.

Because of that story, and how I felt about that story, I was miserable, reactive, resistant, and scared. I was an underachiever, I was a binge eater, and as I got older, I started sleeping around, thinking it was the only way to get a man to love me. I even married a guy so he could get a green card. I spent way more money than I made and ended up declaring bankruptcy. I lashed out at people I loved.

My life wasn't a complete disaster, but I was asleep at the wheel, and I had no idea what was possible for me. I didn't know what I wanted. I didn't know how to desire something for myself.

Having goals and "being responsible" scared me. My anxiety went through the roof. (Funnily enough, it manifested in a severe fear of other people throwing up. It almost paralyzed me, especially in the winter months. There were times when I thought I'd become someone who couldn't leave her home.) This lasted for years. I now understand that I was dealing with post-traumatic stress disorder. I am now also aware that after PTSD can come PTG: post-traumatic growth.

Through various therapies (traditional and not-so-traditional), not to mention reading books about narcissistic mothers and mothers who can't love,

I started to wake up. And while the therapy and the books explained a lot, and helped me feel that I was not alone, they also provided an excuse. The story that stood on me turned into this: Because my mother was and is the way she is, I'm screwed. It's too late for me. I am damaged and that's just the way life happened.

I was most definitely not impressed with myself.

Sure, from time to time I would experience the real, powerful essence of myself, but the stories I'd been telling myself felt permanent and more potent, plus they were familiar. More than anything else, I unconsciously feared that if I was my real self, my mother wouldn't approve of or love me. I certainly had proof of that...and man, if your mother doesn't love you unless you contort yourself to her desires, who will?

Through a combination of writing (it's my number-one therapy) and powerful coaching, over the course of a couple of years I disentangled myself from my mother and from the stories I was telling myself about myself and her. I've come home to myself as a powerful, autonomous woman who understands the nature of true creativity.

Relationships that are important to me (with my husband, my stepchildren, my sister, and my friends) have become healthier and stronger. Why? Because what I used to think of as the "truth" about myself isn't true, and so I no longer act as if it is.

And best of all, I am impressed with the one person who matters most: myself.

I'd be lying if I said that I am done, that I have reached the finish line. When it comes to me and my mother, I will never be done. Now, rather than dread that fact, I relish it. The key to maintaining clarity is continuing to practice the tools.

My mission is to help you impress yourself, get intimate with your triggers, set impeccable boundaries, redefine and renegotiate a healthier adult relationship with your mother (if that's what you want), and ultimately understand your stories so they no longer make you suffer. Perhaps your mother would be interested in doing some of this work, too! Wherever you are on the spectrum is the right place for you to be. And right for your mother, when you extend the thinking.

RECOMMENDED RESOURCES

Here are some suggestions for further exploration...some of which are mentioned in the book and some of which are not:

Mother-Daughter Wisdom by Dr. Christiane Northrup, MD is one of the first books I read on the influence of mothers on their daughters (http://drnorthrup.com).

Other excellent books for daughters are: *Mothers Who Can't Love: A Healing Guide for Daughters* by Dr. Susan Forward, PhD; *Will I Ever Be Good Enough: Healing the Daughter of Narcissistic Mothers* by Dr. Karyl McBride, PhD; and *Adult Children of Emotionally Immature Parents: How to Heal from Distant, Rejecting, or Self-Involved Parents* by Dr. Lindsay Gibson, PsyD.

My go-to source on Victim Consciousness is *Beyond Victim Consciousness* by Lynne Forrest (http://lynneforrest.com).

The work of Maya Angelou stands on its own as inspiration for women everywhere (http://mayaangelou.com).

My go-to source for shadow work is *The Dark Side of the Light Chasers* by Debbie Ford (http://debbieford.com).

Iyanla VanZant's practical wisdom never steers me wrong (http://iyanla.co).

The Language of Emotions by Karla McLaren provides fantastic context and explanation for the wisdom and energy in our emotions (http://karlamclaren.com).

My healthy boundaries guru is Randi Buckley (http://randibuckley.com).

My favorite resource for all things Emotional Freedom Technique (a.k.a. "tapping") is Jondi Whitis (http://eft4results.com/).

For a healthy relationship with your body, I recommend the work of Geneen Roth (http://geneenroth.com), Melissa Toler (http://melissatoler.com), and *The Body Is Not An Apology* movement (http://thebodyisnotanapology.com).

My favorite resource for parents is Dr. Shefali Tsabari, author of *The Conscious Parent: Transforming Ourselves, Empowering Our Children* and *The Awakened Family: A Revolution in Parenting* (http://drshefali.com).

For wisdom and practical magic specific to raising confident tween and teen daughters, I highly recommend the work of Betsy Baird Smith (http://coachbetsy.com/).

Nonviolent Communication: A Language of Life, by Marshall B. Rosenberg, will help improve all your relationships (http://nonviolentcommunication.com/index.htm).

For cultivating creativity, I recommend Laura Munson's Haven Writing Retreats (http://lauramunsonauthor.com/); *Big Magic: Creative Living Beyond Fear*, by Elizabeth Gilbert (http://elizabethgilbert.com); and *The Artist's Way* by Julia Cameron (http://juliacameronlive.com).

For understanding intersectional feminism (not to mention experiencing mind-blowing writing), I recommend the work of Roxane Gay (http://roxanegay.com).

Brené Brown's ground-breaking work in the areas of vulnerability, shame, and resilience will change the way you experience humanity (http://brenebrown.com).

For trauma resolution and healthy sexuality, check out Rachael Maddox, trauma resolution educator, coach, guide, and author of *Secret Bad Girl: A Sexual Trauma Memoir and Resolution Guide* (http://rachaelmaddox.com).

Other excellent resources on trauma are Dr. Bessel Van Der Kolk (http://besselvanderkolk.com) and Dr. Gabor Maté (http://drgabormate.com).

For healthy romantic relationships, look no further than Maggie Reyes and her website, *Modern Married* (http://modernmarried.com).

For healthy divorces, the work of Katherine Woodward Thomas is unparalleled (http://katherinewoodwardthomas.com/)

For more on the concept of the "mother wound," I recommend the work of Bethany Webster (http://womboflight.com).

Without the work of Brooke Castillo, founder of The Life Coach School, I wouldn't be where I am today (http://thelifecoachschool.com).

The work of Martha Beck, especially her book *Diana,*

Herself, will help you reframe any situation in the most delightful of ways (http://marthabeck.com).

The work of Byron Katie, which is actually called "The Work" (http://thework.com), is a great way to question your thoughts.

When it comes to a healthy discussion on death and dying, you can't beat the work of Dr. Martha Atkins, PhD, author of *Sign Posts of Dying* (http://marthaatkins.com).

ACKNOWLEDGEMENTS

I am deeply grateful to the following for their support, encouragement, and inspiration:

Kristen Moeller, fellow seeker and writer, friend, nurturer, and my agent! You believed in me and in my book, and I am forever grateful to you for that.

Brenda, Julie, Sally, Kristen, and Nancy, my Haven Coven Sister Wives.

Laura Munson, who helped me take my writing to a soul level.

Brenda Knight, editor, who shepherded this project.

Cynthia and Dorothy, whom I have no doubt were and will continue to be the perfect mother and grandmother for me. Thank you, Mommy and Grandma, for the life lessons, the struggle, the laughs, the tears, all of it.

Timothy, who didn't love me first, but who loves me best... and who loved me before I knew how to love myself. If I know what love is, it is because of you. Thank you, dearest, sweetest Tim.

ABOUT THE AUTHOR

Karen C. L. Anderson is the founder of *Mare: A Re-Mothering Community* for women. A writer first and master-certified life coach second, Karen believes that the truth never creates suffering and that all stories can be told through the lens of truth. She empowers women to use their voices to tell their truths and reduce their own suffering. In another life, Karen tried to fit her right-brained self into a left-brained career as a trade magazine journalist in the field of plastics (and if she had a dime for every time someone mentioned that line from *The Graduate*...). She is married to a left-brained engineer, and they live in Southeastern Connecticut.

THANK YOU

....

Thank you for reading *Difficult Mothers, Adult Daughters: A Guide For Separation, Inspiration & Liberation*!

Contact Information:

Agent: Waterside Productions Inc.

2055 Oxford Ave.

Cardiff, CA. 92007

Phone: 760-632-9190

Email: admin@waterside.com

Publisher: Mango

Website: http://kclanderson.com/

Facebook: http://facebook.com/KarenCLAnderson/

Twitter: @KCLAnderson

Instagram: KCLAnderson

YouTube: http://youtube.com/karenclanderson